朝花惜拾

Cherished Dawn Blossoms

汉英对照　*中国文学*　书系
A Retrospective of Chinese Literature

中国文学　古代诗歌卷

中国文学出版社 编

外语教学与研究出版社
FOREIGN LANGUAGE TEACHING AND RESEARCH PRESS
中国文学出版社
CHINESE LITERATURE PRESS

图书在版编目(CIP)数据

中国文学：古代诗歌卷/中国文学出版社编.
－北京：外语教学与研究出版社 中国文学出版社,1998.11
(汉英对照 中国文学书系)
ISBN 7－5071－0475－3

Ⅰ.中… Ⅱ.中… Ⅲ.古体诗-中国-古代-选集-对照读物-汉、英
Ⅳ.H319.4：Ⅰ

中国版本图书馆 CIP 数据核字(98)第 32907 号

汉英对照 中国文学书系

中国文学 古代诗歌卷

中国文学出版社 编

外语教学与研究出版社
(北京西三环北路 19 号)
中 国 文 学 出 版 社 出版发行
(北京百万庄路 24 号)

北京外国语大学印刷厂印刷
新华书店总店北京发行所经销

开本 850×1168 1/32 9.75 印张
1998 年 11 月第 1 版 1998 年 11 月第 1 次印刷
1—5000 册

ISBN 7－5071－0475－3/Ⅰ·451
定价：11.90 元

《朝花惜拾》序

　　顾名思义，这是一束再放的花朵。它曾经绽开在大中学生的教材里，摇曳在中文老师的讲义上，灿烂在无数学子的诵读中。春光似水，十年过去，也许五年或十五年，甚而至于更多一些年头，昔日少年已是今天的白领阶层，抑或社会各个阶层各种角色的扮演者，对于曾经在课堂上读过的文章，至今余香在口，每能忆起，那同学少年，那花样季节，那响彻幽雅校园的琅琅之声，无一不令人心醉。于是有一天，我们这一套书的编者便作如是想，假使将那十年前读过的名篇重编一书，新加评注，让旧的读者以新的心境再读一遍，连同已逝的韶华一并温习，不亦乐乎？

　　朝花夕拾是一句美丽的名言，半个世纪以前，它被伟大的四十七岁的鲁迅撷作书名，从此脍炙人口，被人喻为对于旧事的收藏。其实鲁迅斯时尚未到夕，尚以壮年的身心与人奋战正酣，他之所谓朝花乃是儿时，"我有一时，曾经屡次忆起儿时在故乡所吃的蔬菜：菱角，罗汉豆，茭白，香瓜。凡这些，都是极其鲜美可口的；都曾是使我思乡的蛊惑。……惟独在记忆上，还有旧来的意味留存。他们也许要哄骗我一生，使我时时反顾。"我们这一套书的读者当然就更年轻了，虽然你们的"朝"，较之鲁迅那贪吃鲜美可口的罗汉豆的"儿时"略长了几岁，但是你们更是远未到"夕"，仍还处于氤氲而蓬勃的朝气中，因之我们决定变"夕"为"惜"，劝君惜取少年时，劝君惜读当年书，号召年轻的读书人重温学子的旧梦。"旧来的意味"如同初恋，那是要哄骗人的一生，使其时时反顾的，更何况被选入课本的文字，无论诗文小品，也无论古今朝代，大抵都是些大师名作，比罗汉豆们更有咀嚼和回味的价值，这便尤其有惜而拾之的必要了。

　　学而时习之，温故而知新，精通教育的孔子也是这样不倦地教诲着我们。

　　这是编者的第一思想。

　　几乎同时产生的第二思想乃是，将它们配上英文，以作对照，使其兼而成为学习外语的上佳读本，照亮第二类读者的眼睛。我们现在是站在二十一世纪的门口了，作为新世纪的主人，外语是其所必有的素质之一。然而我们是否淡忘，学习外语的初衷恰恰是为了交流，为了共享？有人说二十一世纪是东方的世纪，是中国的世纪，"中国"无疑将是世界一个愈久弥深的话题，那么对世界解说中国，何尝不是埋在我们中国人胸怀的共同愿望。在过去的外语教材中，我们只是读莎士比亚，拜伦，雪莱，狄更斯，司各特，奥斯汀，勃朗特姐妹的《简·爱》和《呼啸山庄》，我们不约而同地忘记了自己的司马迁，屈原，李白，杜甫，苏轼，罗贯中，忘记了全世界最了不起的曹雪芹的《红楼梦》，还有空前绝后的鲁迅和他的天才著作。也未曾想到当我们把伤心的眼泪纷纷抛向英国少女简·爱的时候，大洋彼岸的有情人却正为"质本洁来还洁去"的中国的林妹妹恸哭流涕。假使能有一个聪明的主意，本书系的编者这样想，在学习他国文字的同时也学习了本国文学，即以学习外国语言为直接的目的，而以学习有关中国文化的外语表达为顺带的收获，好比乘坐帆船去一个新鲜的地方，船上却载上了自己故乡的所爱，那简直要叫做一石二鸟了。

但也许有人会这样地认为，学习英语当然还是读英文原著为好，由中文翻译而成的英文能算是地道的英文么？怀疑是大可不必的，本书系的英文译者恰恰大多是母语者，新中国近半个世纪以来，这些英、美等国的文化使者，为了研究神秘的东方文化，他们陆续以外籍语言专家的身份来到中国，在中国文学出版社的安排和中国学者的协同下，从"关关雎鸠，在河之洲"到"灌园叟晚逢仙女"，开始了有着几千年历史的中国文学的系统翻译。而领导这支翻译队伍从事这一伟大工程的，便是驰名中外的中国首席翻译家杨宪益先生和他的英国夫人戴乃迭女士。杨氏夫妇珠联璧合，携手共译的《红楼梦》、《阿Q正传》等中国古今名著，以无可挑剔的艺术水准征服了西方文坛，从此结束了"美文不可译"的神话。

本书系是由享誉海外的中国文学出版社和深受外语学习者信赖的外语教学与研究出版社分工合作、编辑出版的，两家同仁以各自最大的优势联合起来，使即将迈入新世纪的国内出版界有了可行的先例。其奇思异想和大胆设计，想必会得到诸位读者的喝采。

最后，除了喝采，我们还希望听到一些批评的意见，真诚地。

野 莽

1998 年 10 月 5 日匆于听风楼

Cherished Dawn Blossoms
Foreword

Ye Mang

The title of this bilingual collection, *Cherished Dawn Blossoms*, reminds one of a bouquet of reopened blossoms. These blossoms of Chinese literature were once in full bloom in much-read books, in teachers' curricula and on the lips of students. Time flows like water in a river. Ten or more years hence, those students would have grown up, but whatever positions they might hold in society today, they will never forget those beautiful pieces of prose, poetry and stories in their old school books. The sound of the classroom recital of those masterpieces still echo in their ears, making them nostalgic for those school days.

One day, an idea suddenly hit us, the editors of this series — wouldn't it be wonderful to pick up those cherished blossoms and arrange them into bouquets for our readers who would probably look at them again from a new perspective, a matured aesthetic judgment?

"Dawn blossoms plucked at dusk" is a beautifully evocative phrase so familiar to all Chinese people. This is mainly due to Lu Xun, the great man of letters of half a century ago, who published a collection of essays by this title. Since then, it has been used to refer to collections of things of the past. Lu Xun was 47 then and was by no means at the age of "dusk." By "dawn blossoms" he was referring to wonderful things he had seen or experienced when he was a child. He once wrote:

"For a period of time, I often recalled the foods I had eaten when I was a boy, such as water chestnuts, *luohan* beans, *jiaobai*, and *xianggua*. ① All these were extremely delicious. They were the catalysts that triggered my homesickness. . . Only in the memory, do those old sensations still linger. Perhaps they will beguile me all my life, making me look back from time to time."

Most of the readers of this series will probably be much younger than Lu Xun when he wrote those enduring words. But when you were in school, you were maybe only a few years senior than Lu Xun when he savored those flavors of home. However, you may be far from the time of "dusk" — probably still in the prime of life. Therefore, we have decided to change the word "dusk" to "cherished," as their pronunciations are the same in Chinese (*xi*). We would like to remind readers to cherish childhood and cherish the books you read in schools.

The "old sensations" are like first love, which one recalls every now and again. Now that these masterpieces of the past were chosen for text-books — be they a poem or an essay or a short story, from ancient times or of the present — they have given the mind more to chew on than chestnuts or beans. In this sense they are even more precious.

"Isn't it a pleasure to review what one has learned from time to time?" or "To learn something new from reviewing the old." — These are famous lines by Confucius who was an expert in education. This was our first inspiration for compiling this series of books.

The second reason, which arose in our minds almost at the same time as the first, was to include English translations. Reading the

---

① These are foods special to certain areas of China: *luohan* or "arhat" beans are a kind of broad bean, *jiaobai* is from the stem of a wild rice plant, and *xianggu*a or fragrant melon is a fruit similar to a small honeydew melon.

Chinese masterpieces against the English translations, or vice versa, would be a very good way to learn English — or Chinese. As we are now already on the threshold of the twenty-first century, learning other languages is a must for a new generation entering the new century. However, perhaps some of us may have forgotten that the very aim of learning other languages is for communication, for sharing. Some say that the twenty-first century will be the century of the East, the century of China. China has clearly become a hot topic in the world today and will remain so in the future. Then to introduce China to the world and tell people overseas all about us is a common wish of the Chinese people. In the past, we may have read in English-language textbooks, literary works by Shakespeare, Byron, Shelley, Dickens, Scott, Austin, or the Brontë sisters' *Jane Eyre* and *Wuthering Heights*. Maybe some Chinese youth have forgotten about our own Sima Qian, Qu Yuan, Li Bai, Du Fu, Luo Guanzhong, and even Cao Xueqin's *A Dream of Red Mansions*. And what about Lu Xun and his genius works? Perhaps we have not realized that, while we have shed our tears for Jane Eyre, people on the other side of the ocean are weeping over Lin Daiyu.

We are quite certain that reading translations of Chinese literary writings is an easy but effective way to learn another language. At the same time you will review these Chinese masterpieces once more, or learn something new about Chinese culture. This is, as they say, killing two birds with one stone.

English learners may argue that it is better to learn English by reading the works written by natives of Britain and North America. Can an English translation of a piece of Chinese writing be idiomatic? Don't worry — most of the translators of this series have English as their mother tongue. For almost half a century, many English-speaking men and women have come to China, fascinated by what they considered mysterious Eastern culture. Many of them have actually settled in China and joined the editors and translators of the Chinese Literature Press to produce translations of renowned classical to contemporary Chinese literary works. Among them are Yang Xianyi and his wife Gladys Yang who have made pioneering efforts in translation from Chinese into English and have won great admiration the world over. Their skillful translations of *A Dream of Red Mansions*, *The True Story of Ah Q* and other works have enjoyed high prestige in international literary circles.

This series has been jointly compiled and published by the Chinese Literature Press, known internationally for its literary translations of Chinese literature, and the Foreign Language Teaching and Research press, which is popular among foreign language learners for its quality publications throughout China. The two publishing houses have joined forces in publishing this landmark series, which will be doubtlessly beneficial to readers learning English or Chinese who are also interested in Chinese literature.

Finally, we are most grateful to authors of the works included in this series, whether they have long since passed away or are still alive, for giving us the opportunity to cherish this wealth of Chinese literature. We should also thank the translators for rendering them into such beautiful English readings.

October 5, 1998

目　录

4

5

《诗经》中所谓"四始"之一,是描写男子追求所爱女子的四言情歌。以"关关雎鸠,在河之洲"起兴,采用回环复沓形式。表现男子的思慕之情和对爱情的执著追求。"参差"、"窈窕"、"关关"等双声、叠韵、选字的运用,增强了语言的韵律,显得自然、和谐。

关关雎鸠,在河之洲①。
窈窕淑女,君子好逑②。
参差荇菜,左右流之③。
窈窕淑女,寤寐求之④。
求之不得,寤寐思服⑤。
悠哉悠哉,辗转反侧⑥。
参差荇菜,左右采之。
窈窕淑女,琴瑟友之⑦。
参差荇菜,左右芼之⑧。
窈窕淑女,钟鼓乐之⑨。

①关关:雌雄鸟和鸣声。雎(jū 居)鸠(jiū 纠):水鸟名。洲:水中的小块陆地。

②窈(yǎo 咬)窕(tiǎo 朓):漂亮。好(hào 浩)逑(qiú 求):好配偶。逑:雔之借字。雔,双鸟之意。犹匹,结成配偶。

③荇(xìng 杏)菜:水草名。流:采摘。

④寤(wù 误):睡醒。寐(mèi 昧):睡眠。

⑤思服:思念。

⑥悠哉:思虑深长。

⑦琴瑟友之:弹琴鼓瑟,跟她友爱和乐地在一起。

⑧芼(mào 帽):择取。

⑨钟鼓乐之:敲钟击鼓,使她快乐。

Merrily the ospreys cry,
On the islet in the stream.
Gentle and graceful is the girl,
A fit wife for the gentleman.

Short and long the floating water plants,
Left and right you may pluck them.
Gentle and graceful is the girl,
Awake he longs for her and in his dreams.

When the courtship has failed,
Awake he thinks of her and in his dreams.
Filled with sorrowful thoughts,
He tosses about unable to sleep.

Short and long the floating water plants,
Left and right you may gather them.
Gentle and graceful is the girl,
He'd like to wed her, the *qin* and *se*[1] playing.

Short and long the floating water plants,
Left and right you may collect them.
Gentle and graceful is the girl,
He'd like to marry her, bells and drums beating.

---

[1]   Two traditional Chinese musical instruments, rather like the zither; the former has seven strings and the latter twenty-five strings.

这是河边伐木的奴隶所唱的一首抗争之歌。抒发了对奴隶主不劳而获的不满，具有强烈的现实主义精神。全诗分为三章，联章复沓、反复咏唱的形式，既渲染愤激之情，起到深化主题的作用，又展现出周代民歌的音乐性。

坎坎伐檀兮①，置之河之干兮②，河水清且涟猗③。不稼不穑④，胡取禾三百廛兮⑤？不狩不猎，胡瞻尔庭有县貆兮⑥？彼君子兮，不素餐兮⑦！

坎坎伐辐兮⑧，置之河之侧兮，河水清且直猗⑨。不稼不穑，胡取禾三百亿兮⑩？不狩不猎，胡瞻尔庭有县特兮⑪？彼君子兮，不素食兮！

坎坎伐轮兮，置之河之漘兮，河水清且沦猗。不稼不穑，胡取禾三百囷兮？不狩不猎，胡瞻尔庭有县鹑兮？彼君子兮，不素飧兮！

①坎坎：伐木声。

②干：岸。

③猗(yī 衣)：语末助词，犹兮。

④稼：耕种。穑：收获。

⑤廛(chán 蝉)：犹束，捆。

⑥瞻：见，看见。县：即悬字古写。貆(huán 桓)：就是猪獾。

⑦素餐：犹言白吃饭。

⑧辐：车轮上的辐条。

⑨直：指直的波纹。

⑩亿：古时十万为一亿。三百亿言很多。一说亿也是束、捆之意。

⑪特：三岁之兽。

Chop, chop, we cut down the elms
And pile the wood on the bank,
By the waters clear and rippling.
They neither sow nor reap;
How then have they three hundred sheaves of corn?
They neither hunt nor chase;
How then do we see badgers hanging in their courtyards?
Ah, those lords
They do not need to work for their food!

Chop, chop, we cut wood for wheel-spokes
And pile it on the shore,
By the waters clear and flowing.
They neither sow nor reap;
How then have they three hundred stacks of corn?
They neither hunt nor chase;
How then do we see bulls hanging in their courtyards?
Ah, those lords
They do not need to work to eat!

　　坎坎伐檀兮,置之河之干兮,河水清且涟猗。不稼不穑,胡取禾三百廛兮? 不狩不猎,胡瞻尔庭有县貆兮? 彼君子兮,不素餐兮!

　　坎坎伐辐兮,置之河之侧兮,河水清且直猗。不稼不穑,胡取禾三百亿兮? 不狩不猎,胡瞻尔庭有县特兮? 彼君子兮,不素食兮!

　　坎坎伐轮兮,置之河之漘兮^①,河水清且沦猗^②。不稼不穑,胡取禾三百囷兮^③? 不狩不猎,胡瞻尔庭有县鹑兮^④? 彼君子兮,不素飧兮^⑤!

①漘(chún唇):河岸边水土相接处。

②沦:小风吹水面所起的如轮状的波纹。

③囷(qūn逡),圆形粮仓。一说也是束、捆。

④鹑(chún淳):鹌鹑。

⑤飧(sūn孙):熟食。

Chop, chop, we cut hard wood for wheels
And pile it at the river's brink,
By the waters clear and dimpling.
They neither sow nor reap;
How then have they three hundred ricks of corn?
They neither hunt nor chase;
How then do we see quails hanging in their courtyards?
Ah, those lords
They do not have to work to live!

《诗经》开创了中国古代诗歌赋、比、兴的艺术表现手法。赋,即敷陈其事;比,即打比方,以此物比彼物;兴,即先言他物以引起所咏之词,用于一章或一首诗的起头。本诗典型地运用了"比"的手法,将剥削者比作贪婪、可憎的"硕鼠",鲜明而贴切。

硕鼠硕鼠,无食我黍①!
三岁贯女,莫我肯顾②。
逝将去女,适彼乐土③?
乐土乐土,爰得我所④?
硕鼠硕鼠,无食我麦!
三岁贯女,莫我肯德⑤。
逝将去女,适彼乐国?
乐国乐国,爰得我直⑥?
硕鼠硕鼠,无食我苗!
三岁贯女,莫我肯劳⑦。
逝将去女,适彼乐郊?
乐郊乐郊,谁之永号⑧?

①黍:黍子,粘黄米。
②贯:侍奉,供养。女:汝,你。顾:顾念,照顾。
③逝:同誓。去:离去。适:去,往。乐土、乐国、乐郊:均为人们想象中的安乐地方。
④爰:何处。所:安身之所。
⑤德:恩惠,好处。
⑥直:或为职之假,职犹所。
⑦劳:慰劳。
⑧号(háo 毫):叹息,哀叹。

Field mouse, field mouse,
Keep away from our millet!
Three years we have served you
But what do you care about us?
Now we shall leave you
For a happier realm,
A happy realm
Where we shall have a place.

Field mouse, field mouse,
Keep away from our wheat!
Three years we have served you,
But what have you done for us?
Now we shall leave you
For a happier land,
A happy land
Where we shall get our due.

Field mouse, field mouse,
Keep away from our rice shoots!
Three years we have served you,
But have you rewarded us?
Now we shall leave you
For those happy plains,
Those happy plains
Where weeping is never heard.

这是一首弃妇诗，以第一人称口吻，追述女子从与氓相恋、成亲直至被遗弃后的经历。以"桑"比爱情，以桑叶的茂盛和凋零比喻爱情从缠绵到冷淡的变化，形象巧妙地抒发了弃妇的沉痛反思、对负心汉的怨愤之情。

氓之蚩蚩①，抱布贸丝②。
匪来贸丝，来即我谋③。
送子涉淇④，至于顿丘⑤。
匪我愆期⑥，子无良媒。
将子无怒⑦，秋以为期。

乘彼垝垣⑧，以望复关⑨。
不见复关，泣涕涟涟。
既见复关，载笑载言。
尔卜尔筮⑩，体无咎言⑪。
以尔车来，以我贿迁⑫。

①氓(méng 萌)：流民。蚩(chī 痴)蚩：借为嗤嗤，嬉笑貌。一说敦厚貌。

②贸：交易。

③即：接近。谋：商量，指商量婚事。

④淇：卫国地名。

⑤顿丘：卫国地名。

⑥愆(qiān 牵)期：拖延日期。

⑦将(qiāng 枪)：愿，请。

⑧垝(guǐ 诡)垣：即坏墙。

⑨复关：男子住地，代指那男子。一说复，返；关，关卡。复关指那男子返回关卡。

⑩卜：以龟甲占卜。筮(shì 誓)：用蓍(shī 诗)草占卜。

⑪体：指占卜的结果。咎：灾祸，指不吉利。

⑫贿：财物，这里指嫁妆。

A simple fellow, all smiles,
Brought cloth to exchange for thread,
Not in truth to buy thread
But to arrange about me.
I saw you across the Qi
As far as Dunqiu;
It was not I who wanted to put it off,
But you did not have a proper matchmaker.
I begged you not to be angry
And fixed autumn as the time.

I climbed the city wall
To watch for your return to the pass;
And when you did not come
My tears fell in floods;
Then I saw you come,
And how gaily I laughed and talked!
You consulted tortoise-shell and milfoil, ①
And they showed nothing unlucky;
You came with your cart
And took me off with my dowry.

---

① Used for divination.

桑之未落,其叶沃若①。
于嗟鸠兮②,无食桑葚③!
于嗟女兮,无与士耽④!
士之耽兮,犹可说也⑤;
女之耽兮,不可说也。

桑之落矣,其黄而陨。
自我徂尔⑥,三岁食贫⑦。
淇水汤汤⑧,渐车帷裳⑨。
女也不爽⑩,士贰其行⑪。
士也罔极⑫,二三其德⑬!

①沃若:犹沃然,润泽貌。

②于:借为吁。吁嗟是悲叹声。鸠:斑鸠。

③桑葚(shèn 慎):桑树的果实。

④耽(dān 丹):过分的迷恋欢乐。

⑤说:读为脱,解脱之意。

⑥徂(cū 粗):往,指嫁到男家。

⑦三岁:指多年。食贫:犹言受穷吃苦,指过苦日子。

⑧汤(shāng 伤)汤:水盛大貌。

⑨渐:浸湿。帷裳:围住车的幔帐。

⑩爽:过错。

⑪贰(tè 特)其行:贰,"忒"的误字,过错,指男的行为不对。

⑫罔:无,没有。极:准则。

⑬二三其德:指三心二意,不专于爱情。

12

Before the mulberry sheds its leaves,
How green and fresh they are!
Ah, turtle-dove,
Do not eat the mulberries!
Ah, girls,
Do not take your pleasure with men!
A man can take pleasure
And get away with it,
But a girl
Will never get away with it.

The mulberry sheds its leaves
Yellow and sere;
After going to you
Three years I supped on poverty.
Deep are the waters of the Qi;
They wet the curtains as the carriage crossed,
I did no wrong,
You were the one to blame;
It was you who were faithless
And changed.

三岁为妇,靡室劳矣^①;
夙兴夜寐^②,靡有朝矣^③!
言既遂矣,至于暴矣^④。
兄弟不知,咥其笑矣^⑤。
静言思之,躬自悼矣^⑥!

及尔偕老,老使我怨。
淇则有岸,隰则有泮^⑦。
总角之宴^⑧,言笑晏晏^⑨,
信誓旦旦,不思其反^⑩。
反是不思^⑪,亦已焉哉^⑫!

①靡:不,无。
②夙:早。
③靡有朝矣:即朝朝如此。
④言:语助词,无义。遂:犹久。暴:粗暴,虐待。
⑤咥(xì戏):讥笑貌。
⑥言:语助词,无义。躬:身。悼:伤。
⑦隰:应作湿,水名,流经卫地。一说隰(xí席)是低湿之洼地。泮(pàn判):通畔,边际。
⑧总角:未成年男女把头发扎成两角,称总角。这里指未成年之时。宴:快乐。
⑨晏晏:温和貌。
⑩反:即返。
⑪反是不思:过去的事情不再想。
⑫亦已焉哉:犹言算了,罢了。

14

Three years I was your wife,
Never idle in your house,
Rising early and retiring late
Day after day.
All went smoothly
Till you turned rough;
And my brothers, not knowing,
Laughed and joked with me as before.
Alone, thinking over my fate,
I could only lament.

I had hoped to grow old with you,
Now the thought of old age grieves my heart.
The Qi has its shores,
The Shi its banks;
How happy we were, our hair in tufts,[①]
How fondly we talked and laughed,
How solemnly we swore to be true!
I must think no more of the past;
The past is done with —
Better let it end like this!

---

① Young people, before coming of age, tied their hair in two tufts.

这是《国风》中最长的一篇诗作,以叙事为主,兼以抒情,反映了周代奴隶终年劳作却不得温饱的痛苦生活。这首怨刺诗长于运用对比,从衣、食、住三方面对比奴隶与奴隶主的生活,控诉社会的不平。

七月流火①,九月授衣②。一之日觱发③,二之日栗烈④。无衣无褐⑤,何以卒岁!三之日于耜⑥,四之日举趾⑦。同我妇子,馌彼南亩⑧。田畯至喜⑨。

七月流火,九月授衣。春日载阳⑩,有鸣仓庚⑪。女执懿筐⑫,遵彼微行⑬,爰求柔桑⑭。春日迟迟⑮,采蘩祁祁⑯。女心伤悲,殆及公子同归⑰。

①七月:指夏历七月。下文凡说某月均指夏历。流:向下行。火:星名,又称大火,亦即心宿。

②授衣:把赶制冬衣的工作交给妇女做。

③一之日:指周历一月的日子,即夏历十一月的日子,即夏历十一月。下文的二之日、三之日、四之日可以此推出夏历是十二月、正月、二月。觱(bì必)发(bá拔):大风触物之声。

④栗烈:犹言凛冽。

⑤褐:粗毛或粗麻织制的衣服。

⑥于:犹"为",指修理。耜(sì似):一种翻土的农具。

⑦趾:脚,举趾是说举足下田耕种。

⑧馌(yè叶):送饭。

⑨田畯(jùn俊):农官。

⑩载:开始。阳:温暖。

⑪仓庚:鸟名,就是黄莺。

⑫懿筐:深筐。

⑬微行:小道。

⑭爰(yuán元):乃,于是。

⑮迟迟:缓慢貌。

⑯蘩(fán凡):白蒿。祁祁:众多貌。

⑰殆:怕,只怕。公子:国君之子。一说是贵族公子。

In the seventh month Antares sinks in the west,
In the ninth, cloth is handed out for making clothes,
In the eleventh month the wind blows keen,
In the twelfth the weather turns cold;
But without a coat, with nothing warm to wear,
How can we get through the year?
In the first month mend the ploughs,
In the second go out to work
With wives and young ones,
Taking food to the southern fields
To please the overseer.

In the seventh month Antares sinks in the west,
In the ninth, cloth is handed out for making clothes;
As the spring grows warm
And the oriole sings,
The girls taking deep baskets
Go along the small paths
To gather tender mulberry leaves;
As the spring days lengthen
They pluck artemisia by the armful;
But their hearts are not at ease
Lest they be carried off by the lord's son.

①萑(huán 环)：一种芦苇。

②蚕月：就是三月。条桑：为桑树剪枝。

③斨(qiāng 枪)：斧的一种。柄孔方者为斨，圆者为斧。

④远扬：远伸而扬起的枝条。

⑤猗：借为掎(yǐ 椅)，牵引。女桑：嫩桑。

⑥鵙(jú 局)：即伯劳。

⑦载：开始。绩：指纺织。

⑧载：则，这里有"又"之意。玄：红黑色。玄和黄二字作动词用，谓染成玄和黄的颜色。

⑨孔：很。阳：指颜色鲜明。

⑩秀：作动词用，指植物结子。葽(yāo 腰)：草名，即远志。一说可能是油菜。

⑪蜩(tiáo 条)：蝉。

⑫萚(tuò 拓)：草木脱落的叶。

⑬于：为，这里指猎取。貉(hé 河)：俗称狗獾。

⑭同：聚合。指会合人去打猎。

⑮载：则，乃。缵(zuǎn 纂)：继续。武功：指田猎。

⑯私：归私人所有。豵(zōng 宗)：一岁的小猪。这里泛指小兽。

⑰豜(jiān 坚)：三岁的大猪。这里泛指大兽。

七月流火，八月萑苇①。蚕月条桑②，取彼斧斨③，以伐远扬④，猗彼女桑⑤。七月鸣鵙⑥，八月载绩⑦。载玄载黄⑧，我朱孔阳⑨，为公子裳。

四月秀葽⑩，五月鸣蜩⑪。八月其获，十月陨萚⑫。一之日于貉⑬，取彼狐狸，为公子裘。二之日其同⑭，载缵武功⑮，言私其豵⑯，献豜于公⑰。

In the seventh month Antares sinks in the west,
In the eighth, we gather rushes,
In the third, we prune the mulberry,
Taking chopper and bill
To lop off the long branches
And bind up the tender leaves.
In the seventh month the shrike cries,
In the eighth, we twist thread,
Black and yellow;
I use a bright red dye
To colour a garment for the lord's son.

In the fourth month the milkwort is in spike,
In the fifth, the cicada cries;
In the eighth, the harvest is gathered,
In the tenth, down come the leaves;
In the eleventh we make offerings before the chase,
We hunt wild-cats and foxes
For furs for our lord.
In the twelfth month the hunters meet
And drill for war;
The smaller boars we keep,
The larger ones we offer to our lord.

①斯螽（zhōng 终）：蚱蜢。股：腿。

②莎（suō 梭）鸡：纺织娘。振羽：振动翅羽发声。

③宇：屋檐。以上四句的主语都是第四句的蟋蟀。

④穹（qióng 穷）：空隙。窒（zhì志）：堵塞。这句是说堵塞有空隙、漏洞之处，熏走耗子。一说穹是穷究，这句是说找尽鼠洞，堵塞它，熏跑老鼠。

⑤向：朝北的窗。墐（jìn 近）：用泥涂抹。⑥改岁：指过年。

⑦处：住。

⑧郁（yù 玉）：李的一种。薁（yù 玉）：即山葡萄。

⑨亨（pēng 烹）：烹。葵：菜名。菽：豆类。

⑩剥（pū 扑）：打。

⑪介：助。一说是求。眉寿：长寿。

⑫壶：瓠（hù 户）瓜。

⑬叔：拾取。苴（jū 居）：麻子，可食。

⑭荼（tú 途）：苦菜。薪：采柴火。樗（chū 初）：臭椿树。

⑮食（sì 似）：养活。

五月斯螽动股①，六月莎鸡振羽②。七月在野，八月在宇，九月在户，十月蟋蟀入我床下③。穹窒熏鼠④，塞向墐户⑤。嗟我妇子，曰为改岁⑥，入此室处。⑦

六月食郁及薁⑧，七月亨葵及菽⑨。八月剥枣⑩，十月获稻。为此春酒，以介眉寿⑪。七月食瓜，八月断壶⑫，九月叔苴⑬。采荼薪樗⑭，食我农夫⑮。

In the fifth month the locust moves its legs,
In the sixth, the grasshopper shakes its wings,
In the seventh, the cricket is in the fields,
In the eighth, it moves under the eaves,
In the ninth, to the door,
And in the tenth under the bed.
We clear the corners to smoke out rats,
Paste up north windows and plaster the door with mud,
Come, wife and children,
The turn of the year is at hand,
Let us move inside.

In the sixth month we eat wild plums and cherries,
In the seventh we boil mallows and beans,
In the eighth we beat down dates,
In the tenth we boil rice
To brew wine for the spring,
A cordial for the old.
In the seventh month we eat melon,
In the eighth cut the gourds,
In the ninth take the seeding hemp,
Pick lettuce and cut the ailanthus for firewood,
To give our husbandmen food.

①场圃:打谷场地。

②纳:把粮食入仓。

③黍稷重(tóng 同)穋(lù 陆):四种谷物名。

④同:集中。

⑤上:指公家。执:指服差役。宫功:指修建宫室。

⑥于:取。

⑦索:搓制绳索。绹(táo 桃):绳索。

⑧亟:急。乘:登。乘屋,是上房修理屋顶。

⑨其始:指岁始,年初。

⑩冲冲:凿冰声。

⑪凌阴:冰窖。"阴"即"窨"。

⑫蚤:借为早,是一种祭祀仪式。

⑬献羔祭韭:献以羔羊,祭以韭菜。

⑭肃霜:犹言下霜。一说肃霜犹肃爽,指秋高气爽。

⑮朋酒:两樽酒。斯:指示代词,指朋酒。飨(xiǎng 响):以酒食款待人。

⑯跻(jī 讥):登。公堂:当时乡村的公共场所名。

⑰称:端举。兕(sì 似)觥(gōng 工):形如兕牛的酒器。一说是兕牛角做的酒器。

九月筑场圃①,十月纳禾稼②。黍稷重穋③,禾麻菽麦。嗟我农夫!我稼既同④,上入执宫功⑤。昼尔于茅⑥,宵尔索绹⑦。亟其乘屋⑧,其始播百谷⑨。

二之日凿冰冲冲⑩,三之日纳于凌阴⑪。四之日其蚤⑫,献羔祭韭⑬。九月肃霜⑭,十月涤场。朋酒斯飨⑮,曰杀羔羊,跻彼公堂⑯,称彼兕觥⑰,"万寿无疆"!

In the ninth month we repair the threshing-floor,
In the tenth we bring in the harvest,
Millet and sorghum, early and late,
Paddy and hemp, beans and wheat.
There is no rest for farm folk:
Once harvesting is done
We are sent to work in the lord's house;
By day we gather reeds for thatch,
After dusk twist rope,
Then hurry to mend the roofs,
For it is time to sow the many grains.

In the twelfth month we chisel and hew the ice,
In the first, store it away inside cold sheds,
In the second it is brought out
For the sacrifice with lambs and garlic;
In the ninth month the weather is chill,
In the tenth, we sweep and clear the threshing-floor;
With twin pitchers we start the feast,
Killing a young lamb,
Then go up to the hall
And raise the cup of buffalo horn —
"May our lord live for ever and ever!"

这是《湘君》的姊妹篇，为湘水男神的恋歌。本诗想象、构思奇特，以第一人称描写湘君对湘夫人的思慕、对幸福生活的憧憬及候人未遇的惆怅，表达了屈原对美好理想的热烈追求和积极进取精神。有强烈的抒情性，是屈原积极浪漫主义诗歌的代表作。

帝子降兮北渚①，目眇眇兮愁予②。嫋嫋兮秋风③，洞庭波兮木叶下④。登白蘋兮骋望⑤，与佳期兮夕张⑥。鸟何萃兮蘋中⑦，罾何为兮木上⑧？沅有茝兮醴有兰⑨，思公子兮未敢言⑩。荒忽兮远望⑪，观流水兮潺湲⑫。

麋何食兮庭中⑬？蛟何为兮水裔⑭？朝驰余马兮江皋⑮，夕济兮西澨⑯。闻佳人兮召予⑰，将腾驾兮偕逝⑱。筑室兮水中，葺之兮荷盖⑲。荪壁兮紫坛，播芳椒兮成堂。桂栋兮兰橑，辛夷楣兮药房。罔薜荔兮为帷，擗蕙櫋兮既张。白玉兮为镇，疏石兰兮为芳。芷葺兮荷屋，缭之兮杜衡。合百草兮实庭，建芳馨兮庑门。九嶷缤兮并迎，灵之来兮如云。

捐余袂兮江中，遗余褋兮醴浦。搴汀洲兮杜若，将以遗兮远者。时不可兮骤得，聊逍遥兮容与。

①帝子：指湘夫人。相传她是帝尧之女，故称帝子。

②眇眇：极目远视之貌。

③嫋(niǎo鸟)嫋：风微吹貌。

④木叶：树虽。下：落。

⑤白蘋(fán烦)：草名，生于南方湖泽中。骋望：放眼望去。

⑥与佳期：与佳人期，指与湘夫人有期约。夕张：黄昏时有所陈设准备。

⑦萃(cuì翠)：集。蘋(pín贫)：水草。

⑧罾(zēng增)：一种鱼网。

⑨茝(chǎi)，白芷。醴(lǐ里)：同澧，澧水，在今湖南境内流入洞庭湖。

⑩公子：指湘夫人。

⑪荒忽：即恍惚，不明貌。

⑫潺湲：水流不断貌。

⑬麋(mí迷)：兽名，似鹿而大。

⑭蛟：龙的一种，常潜于深水。水裔(yì义)：水涯，水边。

⑮江皋：这里当指水边高地，一说皋是曲泽。

⑯济：渡。澨(shì是)：水涯，水边。

⑰佳人：美人，指湘夫人。

⑱腾：传告，传令。偕逝：同往。

⑲葺(qì气)：用茅草铺盖屋顶，这里指覆盖。荷盖：以荷叶为屋顶。

To the northern bank descends the Lady Goddess;
Sombre and wistful the expression in her eyes.
Sighing softly the autumn breeze;
Leaves fall on the ripples of Dongting Lake.
Amidst the white sedge, I anxiously keep watch
For my love who will come when the sun sets.
Why are the birds flocking in the reeds?
Why are the nets hanging in the trees?
Angelicas by the Yuan and orchids by the Li.
I long for my love but dare not speak my thoughts.
My heart is trembling as I gaze afar
Over the waters which are flowing fast.
Why are the deer browsing in the courtyard?
Why are the dragons cleaving to the bank?
At dawn I ride my horses by the river;
At dusk I cross the current to the western bank.
I shall hear my loved one when he summons me;
Urging my horses I shall speed to his side.
In the river I shall build him a home;
It will have a roof made of lotus leaves,

帝子降兮北渚，目眇眇兮愁予。嫋嫋兮秋风，洞庭波兮木叶下。登白薠兮骋望，与佳期兮夕张。鸟何萃兮蘋中，罾何为兮木上？沅有茝兮醴有兰，思公子兮未敢言。荒忽兮远望，观流水兮潺湲。

麋何食兮庭中？蛟何为兮水裔？朝驰余马兮江皋，夕济兮西澨。闻佳人兮召予，将腾驾兮偕逝。筑室兮水中，葺之兮荷盖。荪壁兮紫坛①，播芳椒兮成堂②。桂栋兮兰橑③，辛夷楣兮药房④。罔薜荔兮为帷⑤，擗蕙櫋兮既张⑥。白玉兮为镇⑦，疏石兰兮为芳⑧。芷葺兮荷屋⑨，缭之兮杜衡⑩。合百草兮实庭⑪，建芳馨兮庑门⑫。九嶷缤兮并迎⑬，灵之来兮如云⑭。

捐余袂兮江中⑮，遗余褋兮醴浦⑯。搴汀洲兮桂若⑰，将以遗远者⑱。时不可兮骤得⑲，聊逍遥兮容与⑳。

①荪（sūn 孙）：香草名，又名溪荪。荪壁，以荪草为墙壁。紫：紫贝。紫坛，以紫贝砌坛。坛，高台或说是庭院。

②播：播撒，散布。成：整。

③桂栋，桂木做的梁。兰橑（liáo 辽），木兰做屋椽。

④辛夷：香木名，楣（méi 眉）：门上的横梁。辛夷楣，以辛夷木做门楣。药：白芷。

⑤罔：同网，动词，编结。帷（wéi 唯）：慢帐。

⑥擗（pǐ 匹）：剖开。櫋（mián 棉）：即室中隔扇。

⑦镇：镇压坐席之物。

⑧疏：分布、陈列。石兰：香草名。

⑨这句说，在荷叶盖的屋顶上又铺上芷。

⑩杜衡：香草名。这句说，在屋的四围又用杜衡绕束。

⑪合：聚集。百草：各种香草，指上文所说的香草。实：充实。

⑫建：陈列，设置。庑（wǔ 武）：廊。一说厢房。

⑬九嶷：九疑山，这里指九疑山之神。缤：盛多貌。

⑭灵：神灵。

⑮捐：弃。袂（mèi 妹）：衣袖。一说袂与下文褋对举，应是夹衣。

⑯遗：丢。褋（dié 蝶）：单衣，楚方言。醴（lǐ 里）：通澧，澧水。袂与褋，当是湘夫人为湘君所缝制，现在要丢弃，是表示决绝。

⑰搴（qiān 千）：拔取，楚方言。汀（tīng 厅）洲：水中平地。杜若：一种香草。

⑱遗（wèi 畏）：赠与。远者：指湘夫人。

⑲时：时机，指相会之时机。骤：屡次。

⑳聊：姑且。容与：舒缓貌。

Iris walls and purple shells for a room.
A hall of fragrant peppers,
Cassia beams and rafters of magnolia,
Jasmine lintels, an arbour of peonies,
And fig-leaves woven into curtains,
Melilotus overhead for a shelter.
White jade stones securing mats,
A screen scented with rock-orchids,
A room of lotus decked with vetch,
And fresh azalea sprigs entwined.
A courtyard filled with wondrous flowers,
Whose fragrance rare assails the gates.
The mountain spirits will greet my love,
Clustering round like clouds.
I dip my sleeve into the waters;
Wash my lapel by the shore of Li.
I pick sweet pollia on an islet,
For my loved one far away.
So rare the precious time we share;
Yet all I can do is wander and wait.

全诗以"哀"为线索，哀郢与自哀相交织，既哀国家危亡，又哀人民苦难；既哀奸佞当道，又哀自己无罪被逐。洋溢全篇的仍是《离骚》中那种爱国主义激情和上下求索的执著追求，感情之深挚怎一个"哀"字了得！

皇天之不纯命兮①，何百姓之震愆②？民离散而相失兮，方仲春而东迁③。

去故乡而就远兮④，遵江夏以流亡⑤。出国门而轸怀兮⑥，甲之鼂吾以行⑦。发郢都而去闾兮，荒忽其焉极⑧，楫齐扬以容与兮⑨，哀见君而不再得⑩。望长楸而太息兮⑪，涕淫淫其若霰⑫。过夏首而西浮兮⑬，顾龙门而不见⑭，心婵媛而伤怀兮⑮，眇不知其所蹠⑯。顺风波以从流兮⑰，焉洋洋而为客⑱。凌阳侯之氾滥兮⑲，忽翱翔之焉薄⑳？心绪结而不解兮㉑，思蹇产而不释㉒。

①皇天：上天。纯命：指天命有常。

②愆（qiān谦）：过失，罪过。震愆，这里指震惊、遭罪。

③迁：迁徙，指逃难。

④故乡：指郢都。就：往。

⑤遵：循，顺着。江夏：指长江和夏水。夏水是古水名，在今湖北省，是长江的分流。

⑥国门：国都之门。轸（zhěn枕）怀：悲痛地怀念。

⑦甲：古代以干支纪日，甲指干支纪日的起字是甲的那一天。鼂（zhāo召）：同朝，早晨。

⑧闾（lú驴）：里巷。里巷是居民区。荒忽：不明貌，指心绪茫然。一说，指行程遥远。焉极：何极，何处是尽头。一说，极，至也。

⑨齐扬：一同举起。容与：行进缓慢。

⑩哀：悲伤。君：指楚王。

⑪楸（qiū秋）：落叶乔木。长楸，高大的楸树。太息：叹息。

⑫涕：泪。淫淫：流泪貌。霰（xiàn现）：雪珠。

⑬过：经过。夏首：地名，在今湖北沙市附近，夏水的起点。西浮：船向西漂行。

⑭顾：回顾，回头看。龙门：郢都的东门。

⑮婵（chán蝉）媛（yuán元）：心绪牵引绵绵貌。

⑯眇：同渺。蹠（zhí直）：践踏，指落脚之处。

⑰顺风波：顺风随水。从流：从流而下。

⑱焉：于是。洋洋：飘飘不定。客：漂泊者。

⑲凌：乘。阳侯：传说中的大波之神，这里指波浪。氾滥：大水横流涨溢。

⑳焉：何。薄：止。

㉑绁（guà挂）：牵挂。结：郁结。解：解开。

㉒蹇（jiǎn简）产：结屈纠缠。释：释然。

High heaven has proved fickle in its bounties;
Why should it frighten our people thus?
Men are scattered and friends separated.
Early in the spring, eastwards we started.
Setting out from my home for places far away;
The Yangtze and Xia were my paths into exile.
With sorrow in my heart, I went through the city gate;
Early on the first day, I commenced my travels.
As I left the city and then my village gate,
An endless despairing seized hold of my mind.
While the boat's oars swished in time,
I mourned for the prince I'd never see again.
A deep sigh escaped me gazing at the forests;
My tears in profusion coursed down like sleet.
Passing the Xia's head, we then drifted westwards,
I searched for the Dragon Gate but all in vain.
Yearning racked my heart and grief my mind;
Going so far away, the path uncertain.
Tossed by wind and waves, aimlessly drifting;
Embarked on an endless journey without hope of return.
Riding the rough waves, these thoughts filled my mind;
When, oh when, will this drifting ever cease?
My heart enmeshed could not be disentangled;
My thoughts trapped in a maze with no escape.

①运舟:行舟。下浮,向下游漂行。

②下江:下入长江。

③终古之所居:犹言祖先世世代代所居住的地方,指郢都。

④逍遥:这里指漂泊。来东:来至东方。

⑤羌:发语词,楚方言,有乃之意。

⑥反:同返。

⑦背:背对着,指离开。夏浦:夏水之滨。西思:思念西方(郢都)。

⑧故都:指郢都。

⑨坟:指水边高地。一说指水边高堤。

⑩聊:姑且。舒:舒展。

⑪州土:这里指楚国州邑乡土。平乐:指和平快乐。

⑫江介:长江两岸。

⑬当:值。陵阳:在今安徽省青阳县,一说,陵阳在今安徽省安庆市东南。焉至:至何处。

⑭淼(miǎo 渺):大水茫茫貌。焉如:何往。

⑮曾(zēng 增)不知:怎不知。夏:同厦,大屋,这里当指楚都之宫殿。丘:丘墟。

⑯孰:谁。一作何。两东门:郢都东南向有二门。

⑰怡:乐。

⑱惟:思,想。一说,惟,发语词。郢路:通向郢都之路。

⑲江:长江。夏:夏水。

将运舟而下浮兮①,上洞庭而下江②。去终古之所居兮③,今逍遥而来东④。羌灵魂之欲归兮⑤,何须臾而忘反⑥?背夏浦而西思兮⑦,哀故都之日远⑧。登大坟以远望兮⑨,聊以舒吾忧心⑩。哀州土之平乐兮⑪,悲江介之遗风⑫。

当陵阳之焉至兮⑬?淼南渡之焉如⑭?曾不知夏之丘兮⑮,孰两东门之可芜⑯!心不怡之长久兮⑰,忧与愁其相接。惟郢路之辽远兮⑱,江与夏之不可涉⑲。忽若不信兮⑳,至今九年而不复㉑。惨郁郁而不通兮㉒,蹇侘傺而含慼㉓。

⑳忽:指时间过得快。信:相信。一说不信是不被信任,下句的不复是不复被信任。

㉑复:指返回郢都。根据句中"九年"的计算,屈原在顷襄王十三年(公元前286年)时被流放,至白起破郢的顷襄王二十一年(公元前278年)首尾正是九年。

㉒郁郁:郁积貌。不通:指心情不通畅。

㉓蹇(jiǎn 简):发语词,楚方言。侘(chà 诧)傺(chì 翅):怅然伫立。慼:同戚,忧伤。

By the current, my boat was borne downstream;
South to the Dongting Lake, north to the river.
My old home abandoned, wherein I had lived,
As I travelled eastwards randomly adrift.
Yet within my soul I burned to return;
Not a moment passed, but I longed to go back.
On leaving Xiapu, my thoughts raced westwards,
Mourning that my city daily grew more distant.
From a hilly island I searched the horizon,
Hoping to relieve the ache within my heart.
But the island's soil so fertile saddened me,
A reminder of the lands beside the Great River.
Where is my destination, as I traverse the water?
How proceed south across this vast waste?
Unaware in my exile the palace had been razed;
Unthinkable the East Gate had crumbled into ruins.
How many are the days since my heart felt joy;
As grief followed sorrow and sorrow followed grief.
Long and hard is the way to the city;
The Yangtze and Xia are difficult to cross.
To have left it seems at times inconceivable;
Yet for nine years I have not been there.
The sadness that blights me is too deep for words;
Chained to that place, life has a bitter taste.

①外：表面。承欢：指承君主之欢。汋(chuò 绰)约：姿态美好貌，一说谄媚之态。

②谌(chén 陈)：诚，实在。荏(rěn 忍)弱：软弱。持：同恃。难持，即是难依靠。

③湛(zhàn 战)湛：厚重貌。

④被：同披。被离，犹披离，纷乱貌。鄣：同障，阻碍，遮蔽。

⑤抗行：高尚伟大的行为。

⑥瞭：目明。杳(yǎo 咬)杳：远貌。薄：近。

⑦被：覆盖，这里犹言加上。不慈之伪名：不慈的恶名。不慈，不爱儿子。尧、舜传位于贤人，不传儿子。

⑧憎：憎恶。愠(wěn 稳)惀(lūn)：忠厚诚朴。修美：修洁美好。

⑨好(hào 号)：爱好，喜欢。夫(fú 扶)人：那些人。忼慨：同慷慨，这里指装腔作势地发表激昂慷慨之言辞。

⑩踥(qiè 妾)蹀(dié 蝶)：小步行走貌，代指小人。

⑪美：美人，指贤人。超远：远。逾迈：犹愈迈，越发远行。

⑫乱：乐章最末段叫乱，后来借用作为辞赋最后总括全篇内容的收尾。

⑬曼：指把眼光放远。流观：四处观览。

⑭冀：希望。一反：即一返，返回一次。

⑮反：同返。

外承欢之汋约兮①，谌荏弱而难持②。忠湛湛而愿进兮③，妒被离而鄣之④，尧舜之抗行兮⑤，瞭杳杳而薄天⑥。众谗人之嫉妒兮，被以不慈之伪名⑦。憎愠惀之修美兮⑧，好夫人之忼慨⑨。众踥蹀而日进兮⑩，美超远而逾迈⑪。

乱曰⑫：曼余目以流观兮⑬，冀一反之何时⑭？鸟飞反故乡兮⑮，狐死必首丘⑯。信非吾罪而弃逐兮⑰，何日夜而忘之⑱！

⑯首丘：头向着所居住生长的山丘。

⑰信：确实。弃逐：指放逐。

⑱之：指故乡郢都。

Your favour was won by outward flattery;
Too weak to resist, without independent will.
When I, most loyal, tried to approach you,
Envy triumphed and obstructed me.
Yao and Shun so renowned for noble deeds,
That their glory was even reflected in the skies;
Yet many vicious tongues, jealous of their fame,
Spread ugly slanders and said they were not good.
Now you abhor the patient quest for beauty,
Preferring instead a scoundrel's trumpeting.
The mobs swarm round, each day closer in your favour;
While beauty spurned withdraws far away.

Envoi

So long have my eyes stared into the distance;
Yearning once to return, but never knowing when.
The birds can fly home to their old nests;
The dying fox can turn to face his earth.
That I was blameless, yet cast aside and exiled;
Each day and night this still sears my soul.

本诗连用自然界不可能出现的五种现象发誓,大胆、直率地表白自己对爱情的坚贞。感情真挚浓烈,语言朴素动人。尽管后世文人竞相仿作,但也只有唐民间曲子词中的"枕前发尽千般愿:要休且待青山烂,水面上秤锤浮,直待黄河彻底枯。……"(《菩萨蛮》)可与之媲美。

上邪①!我欲与君相知②,长命无绝衰③。山无陵④,江水为竭,冬雷震震,夏雨雪⑤,天地合,乃敢与君绝!

①上邪:犹言"天啊"。
②相知:相爱。
③命:古与"令"字通,使。
④陵:山峰。
⑤雨雪:降雪。

By heaven,
I shall love you
To the end of time!
Till mountains crumble,
Streams run dry,
Thunder rumbles in winter,
Snow falls in summer,
And the earth mingles with the sky —
Not till then will I cease to love you!

汉乐府叙事诗中脍炙人口的名篇。集中笔墨刻划了一个劳动妇女罗敷的形象,以夸张、铺陈和侧面烘托等手法,展现了她的容貌美和人格美;讽刺了使君的粗鄙和狂妄。有浓郁的浪漫主义色彩,其艺术手法明显地影响到辛延年《羽林郎》、曹植《美女篇》的创作。

①隅:方。

②罗敷:采桑女的名字。

③蚕桑:指采桑养蚕。

④青丝:青色的线绳。笼:篮子。系:系篮子的绳。

⑤钩:篮上的提柄。

⑥倭堕髻:即堕马髻。

⑦明月珠:宝珠名,产于大秦国(罗马帝国)。

⑧缃(xiāng 湘):浅黄色。绮(qǐ 起):有花纹的丝织品。

⑨襦(rú 儒):短袄。

⑩下担:放下担子。捋(lǚ 吕):顺着抚摩。髭(zī 资)须:胡子。

⑪帩(qiào 俏)头:即绡头,古代男子包头发的纱巾。

⑫但:只是。坐:因为。

日出东南隅①,照我秦氏楼。秦氏有好女,自名为罗敷②。罗敷喜蚕桑③。采桑城南隅。青丝为笼系④,桂枝为笼钩⑤。头上倭堕髻⑥,耳中明月珠⑦。缃绮为下裙⑧,紫绮为上襦⑨。行者见罗敷,下担捋髭须⑩。少年见罗敷,脱帽著帩头⑪。耕者忘其犁,锄者忘其锄。来归相怨怒,但坐观罗敷⑫。

使君从南来,五马立踟蹰。使君遣吏往,问是谁家姝。"秦氏有好女,自名为罗敷。""罗敷年几何?""二十尚不足,十五颇有余。""使君谢罗敷,宁可共载否?"罗敷前置辞:"使君一何愚!使君自有妇,罗敷自有夫。"

"东方千余骑,夫婿居上头。何用识夫婿?白马从骊驹;青丝系马尾,黄金络马头;腰中鹿卢剑,可直千万余。十五府小吏,二十朝大夫,三十侍中郎,四十专城居。为人洁白皙,鬑鬑颇有须。盈盈公府步,冉冉府中趋。坐中数千人,皆言夫婿殊。"

The morning sunlight
Shines on the Qin mansion
Whose pride is the lady,
The lady Luofu.
For the silkworms she tendeth
She strippeth the mulberries
Which grow to the south;
From the cassia her basket
Hangs by a silk ribbon;
She has hair neatly braided,
Pearl earrings like moonbeams,
Silk petticoat yellow
And apron of purple.
When a wayfarer sees her
He sets down his burden
Awhile, strokes his beard.
A youth when he sees her
Doffs cap and salutes.
The ploughman leaves ploughing,
The hoer his hoeing,
And back in their houses

日出东南隅,照我秦氏楼。秦氏有好女,自名为罗敷。罗敷喜蚕桑。采桑城南隅。青丝为笼系,桂枝为笼钩。头上倭堕髻,耳中明月珠。缃绮为下裙,紫绮为上襦。行者见罗敷,下担捋髭须。少年见罗敷,脱帽著帩头。耕者忘其犁,锄者忘其锄。来归相怨怒,但坐观罗敷。

使君从南来①,五马立踟蹰②。使君遣吏往,问是谁家姝③。"秦氏有好女,自名为罗敷。""罗敷年几何?""二十尚不足,十五颇有余。""使君谢罗敷④,宁可共载否⑤?"罗敷前置辞⑥:"使君一何愚⑦!使君自有妇,罗敷自有夫。"

"东方千余骑,夫婿居上头。何用识夫婿?白马从骊驹;青丝系马尾,黄金络马头;腰中鹿卢剑,可直千万余。十五府小吏,二十朝大夫,三十侍中郎,四十专城居。为人洁白皙,鬑鬑颇有须。盈盈公府步,冉冉府中趋。坐中数千人,皆言夫婿殊。"

①使君:当时对太守、刺史的称呼。

②五马:汉朝太守有用五马驾车的。踟蹰:徘徊不前貌。

③姝:美女。

④谢:谦词。这里是问的意思。

⑤宁(nìng佞)可:犹言愿意,情愿。共载:同乘一车。

⑥置辞:致辞,答话。

⑦一:语助词,有加强语气的作用。何:多么。

Find fault with their wives,
Having gazed on Luofu.

From the south comes a lordling
In carriage with five horses;
Surprised, halts and sends one
To make an inquiry,
"Who is that beauty,
And who are her kin?"
"She is one of the Qins,
And her name is Luofu."
"And what may her age be?"
"Her summers not twenty,
Yet more than fifteen."
Then he, condescending,
Says, "Luofu, will't please you
To enter my carriage?"
She faces him boldly,
And thus makes reply:

"What nonsense you talk, sir!
You have your own wife,
And I my own husband.

①上头:行列的前头。

②骊驹:纯黑的小马。

③系(jì 记):绾结。络:络头,这里用作动词,上着络头。

④鹿卢:一般写作辘轳,井上汲水的滑轮。剑柄上用绦带缠绕,形似辘轳的剑称鹿卢剑。

⑤直:同值。

⑥府小吏:太守府的小吏。

⑦朝大夫:朝廷的大夫。大夫是官名。

⑧侍中郎:官名,皇帝的侍从官。

⑨专城居:这里指太守。

⑩为:其。为人,其人也。皙(xī 西):白。

⑪鬑(lián 连)鬑:鬓发长貌。这里指胡须长。

⑫盈盈:步履轻盈貌。公府步:指做官人走路的步伐。

⑬冉冉:行步舒缓貌。

⑭殊:突出,与众不同。

日出东南隅,照我秦氏楼。秦氏有好女,自名为罗敷。罗敷喜蚕桑。采桑城南隅。青丝为笼系,桂枝为笼钩。头上倭堕髻,耳中明月珠。缃绮为下裙,紫绮为上襦。行者见罗敷,下担捋髭须。少年见罗敷,脱帽著帩头。耕者忘其犁,锄者忘其锄。来归相怨怒,但坐观罗敷。

使君从南来,五马立踟蹰。使君遣吏往,问是谁家姝。"秦氏有好女,自名为罗敷。""罗敷年几何?""二十尚不足,十五颇有余。""使君谢罗敷,宁可共载否?"罗敷前置辞:"使君一何愚!使君自有妇,罗敷自有夫。"

"东方千余骑,夫婿居上头①。何用识夫婿?白马从骊驹②;青丝系马尾③,黄金络马头;腰中鹿卢剑④,可直千万余⑤。十五府小吏⑥,二十朝大夫⑦,三十侍中郎⑧,四十专城居⑨。为人洁白皙⑩,鬑鬑颇有须⑪。盈盈公府步⑫,冉冉府中趋⑬。坐中数千人,皆言夫婿殊⑭。"

From the east ride a thousand
With him at their head.
And how shall you know him?
By the white horse he rides,
By the black colt that follows,
Their silk-braided tails
And their gold-braided halters;
By the sword at his side,
With its hilt of jade fashioned,
For which he paid millions.
At the age of fifteen
He kept prefecture minutes,
A scribe in his twenties,
At thirty a minister;
Now, being forty,
He governs a district.
His skin is so fair
And he wears a long beard.
He moves in the *yamen*
With step slow and stately;
He sits among thousands
Who own him their best. "

汉乐府的突出特色在其叙事性，很多篇章都有故事情节和人物肖像、心理、语言、动作、细节的描写。《东门行》正是截取了故事发展高潮时的片断，通过夫妻的对话，表现丈夫因穷困所迫，铤而走险的家庭悲剧，维妙维肖的动作、质朴传神的口吻使人物形象跃然纸上。

出东门，不顾归①。来入门，怅欲悲。盎中无斗米储②，还视架上无悬衣③。拔剑东门去，舍中儿母牵衣啼④："他家但愿富贵，贱妾与君共铺糜⑤。上用仓浪天故⑥，下当用此黄口儿⑦。今非⑧！""咄⑨！行！吾去为迟！白发时下难久居⑩。"

①顾：思，念。

②盎(àng)：肚大口小的瓦罐。

③还视：回视，回首看。

④儿母：指主人公的妻子。

⑤铺：吃。糜：粥。

⑥用：因。仓浪天：苍天。故：缘，缘由。

⑦黄口儿：幼儿。

⑧今非：是说今去铤而走险不对。

⑨咄(duō 多)：指丈夫因妻子一再劝阻而发出的埋怨声。

⑩这四句是说我要走了！我现在出门都已经晚了！我头上的白发已不时地脱落，实难再在家久待了！

Outside the eastern gate
He hardly dare go home;
Once over the threshold,
He chokes with grief again:
Not a peck of rice left in the pot,
Not a coat on the peg behind. . .
Sword in hand he starts back to the eastern gate,
But his wife clutches at his sleeve and weeps.

"Others may hanker after rank and riches,
I am content to share your gruel with you.
By the blue sky above,
Think of your unweaned child!
Do not do this thing!"

"Bah! Let me go!
Already it is too late.
Are we to drag on like this
Till our hair is white?"

汉乐府中现实主义与浪漫主义相结合的代表作。体现了汉乐府"感于哀乐、缘事而发"的特点。本诗采用第三人称讲述了刘兰芝与焦仲卿的爱情悲剧，注重以语言描写、细节描写、动作描写突出人物形象，使情节完整，叙述性增强，标志着古代叙事诗的发展和成熟。

①建安：东汉献帝年号（公元196年－公元219年）。

②庐江：汉郡名，郡治始在今安徽省庐江县西南，汉末徙至今安徽省潜山县。

③徘徊：往返回旋貌。以上二句以孔雀向东南飞去，但因留恋配偶而徘徊顾盼起兴，引起下文对焦仲卿、刘兰芝的爱情悲剧的叙述。

④素：白色的绢。

⑤箜（kōng 空）篌（hóu 喉）：古代的一种拨弦乐器。

⑥守节：坚持做官的职守。一说守节指刘兰芝的爱情忠贞不移。一本此句下有"贱妾留空房，相见常日稀"二句。故诗中二句是说，你在外为官，令我常守空房，但我坚守节操，坚贞不移。

汉末建安中①，庐江府小吏焦仲卿妻刘氏②，为仲卿母所遣，自誓不嫁。其家逼之，乃投水而死。仲卿闻之，亦自缢于庭树。时人伤之，而为此辞也。

孔雀东南飞，五里一徘徊③。"十三能织素④，十四学裁衣，十五弹箜篌⑤，十六诵诗书。十七为君妇，心中常苦悲。君既为府吏，守节情不移⑥。鸡鸣入机织，夜夜不得息。三日断五匹⑦，大人故嫌迟⑧。非为织作迟，君家妇难为。妾不堪驱使，徒留无所施⑨。便可白公姥⑩，及时相遣归⑪。"

⑦断：裁断，剪断。

⑧大人：这里指仲卿之母。

⑨妾：古代妇女自称的谦词。施：用。

⑩白：禀告。公姥（mǔ 母）：公婆，下文未提及公公，所以特指婆母。

⑪遣归：休弃回家。

Jiao Zhongqing was a local official in the Prefecture of Lujiang during the reign of Jianan (AD 196-219) in the Eastern Han Dynasty. His wife Liu was sent away by his mother and vowed never to marry again. Compelled by her family to break her vow, she had no recourse but to drown herself in a pond. On receipt of the news Jiao Zhongqing hanged himself in his courtyard. The long poem was composed by their contemporaries in their memory.

Southeast the love-lorn peacock flies. Alack,
At every mile she falters and looks back!
At thirteen years Lanzhi learned how to weave;
At fourteen years she could embroider, sew;
At fifteen music on her lute she made;
At sixteen knew the classics, prose and verse,
At seventeen they wed her to Zhongqing,
And from that day what joy and pain were hers!
As work kept Zhongqing in the *yamen* far,
His absence made her love the deeper still.
She started weaving at the dawn of day,
Worked at the loom until the midnight hour.
The tapestries beneath her fingers grew,
Yet Zhongqing's mother sore berated her —
Not for poor work or any tardy pace,
But she was mistress: brides must know their place.

At length in sorrow to Zhongqing she said,
"If I have failed to serve your mother well,
Useless to stay... Please go and tell her so.
Should she think fit, I fain would go away."

①启：启禀，告禀。

②薄禄：做小官拿微薄的俸禄。相：命相。

③共事：指夫妻共同生活。尔：这样，指夫妻生活。

④行：行为。偏斜：不正当，出差错。

⑤何意：哪想到，何曾料到。不厚：这里犹言不喜欢。

⑥区区：小。这里指见识短浅。

⑦自专由：这里是自作主张，举动任性之意。

⑧可怜：可爱。体：体态相貌。

⑨伏惟：本意是伏地而思。古人下对上陈述意见时常以此二字开头，表示自己的谦卑和对听话人的尊敬。

⑩取：同娶。

⑪床：古时的一种坐具。不是今天的卧具。

⑫会：必定，坚决。

府吏得闻之，堂上启阿母①："儿已薄禄相②，幸复得此妇。结发同枕席，黄泉共为友。共事二三年，始尔未为久③。女行无偏斜④，何意致不厚⑤？"阿母谓府吏："何乃太区区⑥！此妇无礼节，举动自专由⑦。吾意久怀忿，汝岂得自由？东家有贤女，自名秦罗敷。可怜体无比⑧，阿母为汝求。便可速遣之，遣去慎莫留！"府吏长跪告，伏惟启阿母⑨："今若遣此妇，终老不复取⑩！"阿母得闻之，槌床便大怒⑪："小子无所畏，何敢助妇语！吾已失恩义，会不相从许⑫！"

The husband, shame-faced, on this errand went.
"Mother," he said, "no lordly post is mine.
To wed Lanzhi was more than I deserved.
As man and wife we love each other so
That naught but death itself shall sever us.
Less than three years have we been wedded now;
Our life together is a budding flower.
Lanzhi methinks, has done her best, no less.
Why treat her, then, with such unkindliness?"

To which the shrewish mother made reply,
"Dull are your wits and foolish, O my son!
Your wife lacks graces and she lacks good sense.
See her for what she is, self-willed and vain.
The very sight of her offends my eyes.
I wonder that you dare to plead her cause!
A proper wife I have in mind for you...
Yonder she lives, a maid called Qin Luofu,
A matchless beauty, upon my word,
And I have ways to compass her consent.
Now listen! We must get your slut away!
Yes, go must she, and go without delay!"

For filial piety he knelt down,
And pitiful yet firm was his appeal.
"Mother, if 'tis your will, cast out Lanzhi,
But do not think that I will marry twice!"
At this the mother's fury knew no bounds.
She ranted wildly, strumming on her stool:

府吏默无声,再拜还入户。举言谓新妇,哽咽不能语:"我自不驱卿①,逼迫有阿母。卿但暂还家,吾今且报府②。不久当归还,还必相迎取③。以此下心意④,慎勿违吾语。"

①卿:古时君称臣以及平辈之间互称卿,丈夫对妻子亦可爱称为卿。

②报府:赴府报到。

③相迎取:去迎接你回来。

④下心意:安心,放心。一说指低声下气。

48

"Is reverence for aged parents dead?
Defend a wife and flout a mother's wish?
This stranger in the house I will not bear,
And none henceforth to thwart my will shall dare!"

Zhongqing fell dumb before his mother's rage,
Made her a bow profound and went his way.
In tears and sorrow he sought poor Lanzhi,
Though little comfort for them both he knew.
"The thought of parting rends my heart in twain!
And yet my mother will not be gainsaid.
My duties at the *yamen* call me hence.
'Tis best you go back to your brother's home.
My *yamen* tasks complete, I will return
And take you with me to our home again.
It has to be, alas! Forgive me now,
And doubt not I will keep my solemn vow!"
Lanzhi made answer sorrowful and low:
"Nay, take no care to come for me again.
'Twas in the depth of winter, I recall,
I first came to this house a timid bride.
I bore myself with filial reverence,
Was never obstinate, self-willed or rude.

新妇谓府吏:"勿复重纷纭①! 往昔初阳岁②,谢家来贵门③。奉事循公姥④,进止敢自专⑤? 昼夜勤作息⑥,伶俜萦苦辛⑦。谓言无罪过,供养卒大恩。仍更被驱遣,何言复来还? 妾有绣腰襦⑧,葳蕤自生光⑨。红罗复斗帐⑩,四角垂香囊。箱帘六七十⑪,绿碧青丝绳。物物各自异,种种在其中。人贱物亦鄙⑫,不足迎后人⑫。留待作遗施⑬,于今无会因⑭。时时为安慰,久久莫相忘。"

①重:再。纷纭:纷扰,麻烦。

②初阳岁:阳气初动之时。指阴历十一月。

③谢家:辞家。

④奉事:行事。循:顺从。

⑤进止:举止。

⑥作息:工作休息,这里指工作。

⑦伶(líng 铃)俜(pīng 乒):孤独貌。萦:围绕,缠绕。

⑧绣腰襦(rú 儒):绣花短袄。

⑨葳(wēi 威)蕤(ruí):草木下垂貌。这里指所绣的花样,花叶繁茂,光彩闪烁。

⑩罗:一种丝织品。复斗帐:双层的床帐。

⑪帘:读为奁(lián 帘),古代盛梳妆用品的匣子。

⑫后人:指仲卿再娶的后妻。

⑬遗(wèi 畏)施:赠送。作遗施,犹言作为赠送施舍给别人的东西。

⑭无会因:没有见面的机会。

For three years, day and night, I toiled for her,
Nor heeded how long that sorry state might last,
My only care to serve your mother's will
And to repay the love you bore to me.
Yet from this house I now am driven out . . .
To what avail to bring me back again?
I'll leave my broidered jacket of brocade,
(Its golden lacings still are fresh and bright,)
My small, soft canopy of scarlet gauze
With perfumed herbs sewn in its corners four.
My trunks, my dowry, too, I leave behind,
As fair as ever in their silken wraps —
Things, some of them, I had a fancy for,
Though now neglected and untouched they lie.
True, they are only cheap and tawdry wares,
Not nearly good enough for your new bride.
But you may share them out as tiny gifts,
Or, if you find no fit occasion now,
Keep them, my dear," she said, her eyes all wet,
"And her who owned them do not quite forget."

When the loud cock-crow marked another day
Lanzhi arose betimes and dressed herself.
She put on her embroidered skirt of silk,
And silken slippers pleasing to the eye,
Studded her braided locks with jewellery,
Hung pearly earrings in her little ears,
With touch so delicate applied the rouge
Until her lips, already perfect, glowed.

鸡鸣外欲曙，新妇起严妆①。著我绣袄裙②，事事四五通③。足下蹑丝履④，头上玳瑁光⑤。腰若流纨素⑥，耳著明月珰⑦。指如削葱根，口如含朱丹⑧。纤纤作细步，精妙世无双。上堂谢阿母，母听去不止⑨。"昔作女儿时，生小出野里，本自无教训，兼愧贵家子。受母钱帛多⑩，不堪母驱使。今日还家去，念母劳家里。"却与小姑别⑪，泪落连珠子："新妇初来时，小姑始扶床，今日被驱遣，小姑如我长。勤心养公姥，好自相扶将⑫。初七及下九⑬，嬉戏莫相忘。"出门登车去，涕落百余行。

①严妆：郑重的打扮。

②著(zhuó 灼)：着，穿着。袄(jiá 夹)裙：双层的的裙。

③四五通：犹言四五遍。

④蹑：踩，这里指穿鞋。丝履：用丝织品做的鞋。

⑤玳(dài 代)瑁(mào 冒)：用玳瑁(一种龟类，其壳可做装饰品)做的头饰。

⑥纨素：精致的白色绢。这句是说兰芝腰间系着的纨素盈若流水。一说若字是着字之误。

⑦珰(dāng 当)：耳环。明月是指叫作明月珠的宝珠。

⑧朱丹：一种红色宝石。女子唇涂口红，故言"口如含朱丹"。

⑨不止：不阻止。这句是说婆母听兰芝自去而不加留止。

⑩钱帛：这里指聘礼。

⑪却：再，还。

⑫扶将：扶持帮助哥哥持家。

⑬初七：指七月初七，这天晚上妇女供祭织女，乞巧。下九：古代每月二十九日叫上九，初九为中九，十九日为下九。下九晚上妇女停止劳作，聚在一起游戏，叫阳会。

Her fingers had a tapering loveliness,
Her waist seemed like a many-coloured cloud.
A peerless beauty did she look, and sweet
The grace with which she moved her little feet.
To Zhongqing's mother then she bade farewell
In tender words that found a churlish ear:
"Lady, I am of humble origin,
Not well instructed and not well brought-up.
Stupid and shallow and inept am I —
A sorry mate for any noble heir.
Yet you have treated me with kindliness,
And I, for shame, have not served you well.
This house for evermore today I leave,
And that I cannot serve you more I grieve."
Then, trickling down her cheeks warm tears,
She bade farewell to Zhongqing's sister dear:
"When to this house I first came as a bride,
Dear sister, you were just a naughty child.
See, you have grown well nigh as tall as I.
Now I must bid a hasty, long farewell;
Yet, if you love me, sister, for my sake,
Be gentle to your mother, care for her.
When all the maidens hold their festivals,
Forget not her who once looked after you."
With blinding tears and with a heavy heart
She took her seat then in the waiting cart.

府吏马在前,新妇车在后,隐隐何甸甸①,俱会大道口。下马入车中,低头共耳语:"誓不相隔卿②,且暂还家去,吾今且赴府。不久当还归,誓天不相负。"新妇谓府吏:"感君区区怀③。君既若见录④,不久望君来。君当作磐石⑤,妾当作蒲苇⑥。蒲苇纫如丝⑦,磐石无转移。我有亲父兄⑧,性行暴如雷,恐不任我意,逆以煎我怀⑨。"举手长劳劳⑩,二情同依依⑪。

①隐隐、甸甸:车声。

②隔:断绝情义。

③区区:爱慕,诚挚。

④录:记住,记得。见录,犹言承蒙你记得。

⑤磐(pán 盘)石:厚重的石头。比喻爱情坚贞不移。

⑥蒲:一种可制席的水生植物。苇:芦苇。比喻虽柔弱但坚韧。

⑦纫(rèn 认):同韧。

⑧父兄:下文未提兰芝之父,因此特指其兄。

⑨逆:违背。煎我怀:犹言使我内心痛苦如煎。

⑩举手:举手告别。劳劳:惆怅忧伤貌。

⑪依依:恋恋不舍貌。

For fear of prying eyes and cruel tongues
Zhongqing would meet her where the four roads met.
On the rough road her carriage pitched and shook,
The wheel-rims clattered and the axle creaked.
Then suddenly a horseman galloped up,
Down leaped the rider eagerly — 'twas he!
They sat together and he whispered low:
"My love shall last to all eternity!
Only a short while with your brother stay,
The little while my *yamen* duties take.
Then I'll come back... Let not your heart be sore!
I'll claim you for my very own once more!"

Poor Lanzhi, sobbing, fondly plucked his sleeve.
"Oh, what a comfort to me is your love!
And if you cannot bear to give me up,
Then come, but come before it is too late!
Be your love strong, enduring as the rocks!
Be mine resistant as the creeping vine!
For what is tougher than the creeping vine?
And what more fixed than the eternal rocks?
Yet when I think upon my brother, lord
And tyrant of his household, then I fear
He will not look on me with kindliness,
And I shall suffer from his rage and scorn."
At length in tears the loving couple parted,
And lengthening distance left them broken-hearted.

入门上家堂,进退无颜仪①。阿母大拊掌②:"不图子自归③!十三教汝织,十四能裁衣,十五弹箜篌,十六知礼仪,十七遣汝嫁,谓言无誓违④。汝今无罪过,不迎而自归?"兰芝惭阿母⑤:"儿实无罪过。"阿母大悲摧⑥。

①无颜仪:犹言脸上觉得无光,难为情。

②拊(fǔ府)掌:拍手。惊讶的动作。

③不图:没料到,没想到。

④誓:疑为謇(qiān 千)字之误。謇是愆的古字。愆违即过失意。

⑤惭阿母:惭愧地回答母亲。

⑥悲摧:悲痛伤心。

When Lanzhi, all unheralded, reached home,
Doubt and suspicion clouded every mind.
"Daughter!" her mother in amazement cried.
"Alas! What brings you unattended back!
At thirteen, I recall, you learned to weave;
At fourteen you could embroider, sew;
At fifteen, music on the lute you made;
At sixteen knew the classics, prose and verse.
And then at seventeen, a lovely bride...
How proud I was to see you prosper so!
Yet, dear, you must have erred in deed or word.
Tell me the cause of your return alone."
Said Lanzhi, "Truly I am brought full low,
Yet in my duty did I never fail."
The mother wept for pity at her tale.

还家十余日,县令遣媒来。云"有第三郎,窈窕世无双,年始十八九,便言多令才①。"阿母谓阿女:"汝可去应之。"阿女衔泪答②:"兰芝初还时,府吏见丁宁③,结誓不别离。今日违情义,恐此事非奇④。自可断来信⑤,徐徐更谓之⑥。"阿母白媒人:"贫贱有此女,始适还家门⑦;不堪吏人妇,岂合令郎君?幸可广问讯⑧,不得便相许。"

①便(pián骈)言:有口才,善辞令。令才:美好的才能。

②衔泪:含泪。

③丁宁:即叮咛,反复嘱咐。

④奇:佳,好。

⑤断:断绝,回绝。信:使者,这里指媒人。

⑥这句犹言慢慢再说吧。

⑦适:出嫁。还家门:指被休弃回家。

⑧幸:希冀,希望。广问讯:多方打听。

Upon the tenth day after her return
There came one from the county magistrate,
A go-between, to woo her for his son,
A lad who had bare twenty summers seen,
Whose good looks put all other youths to shame,
Whose tongue was fluent and full eloquent.
Her mother, hoping against hope, said, "Child,
I pray you, if it pleases you, consent."
To which, in tears again, Lanzhi replied:
"Dear mother, when I parted with Zhongqing
He said, 'Be faithful!' o'er and o'er again,
And we both vowed eternal constancy.
If I should break my word and fickle prove,
Remorse would haunt me till my dying day.
Can I then think to wed again? No, no!
I pray you tell the matchmaker so."
So to the go-between the mother said:
"O honoured sir, a stubborn child is mine,
But lately sent back to her brother's house.
A small official found her no good match —
How should she please the magistrate's own heir?
Besides, she is in melancholy state:
Young gentlemen require a gayer mate."
So the official go-between went off
And, ere reporting to the magistrate,
Found for the sprig another fitting maid,
Born of a nearby family of note;
And, haply meeting with the Prefect's scribe,
Learned that His Excellency's son and heir,

①寻:不久。丞:指县丞。请:指向郡守请示工作。还:指县丞回县。这句是说过了不久,被县令派去向太守请示工作的县丞回县了。

②承籍:继承先辈的仕籍。以上二句是县丞对县令所说的话,建议他向刘家求婚,说有个兰家的女子,家里继承先的仕籍,是为官作宦的人家。

③娇逸:娇好而文雅。

④主簿:郡、县府里掌文书档案的官吏。通语言:指传达话。以上四句还是县丞对县令所说的话,告诉他太守的第五个儿子娇美而文雅,还未结婚,太守派县丞作媒人,而传达太守意见的是郡府里的主簿。

⑤结大义:指结为婚姻。

⑥贵门:对人家的敬称。以上四句是县丞来刘家说媒的话。

⑦老姥:刘母自称。

⑧作计:作决定,打主意。不量:不思量,欠考虑。

⑨否(pǐ痞)泰:指坏运气和好运气。这句是说好坏相差有如天地之别。

⑩义郎:对男子的美称。其往:往后,将来。何云:说什么,这里是怎么办,如何打算的意思。

⑪处分:处理,决定。适:顺从。

⑫要(yāo腰):约,立下誓言。

⑬渠:那种。无缘:没有机会。

⑭登即:当即,立即。

媒人去数日,寻遣丞请还①,说"有兰家女,承籍有宦官②。"云"有第五郎,娇逸未有婚③,遣丞为媒人,主簿通语言④。"直说"太守家,有此令郎君,既欲结大义⑤,故遣来贵门⑥。"阿母谢媒人:"女子先有誓,老姥岂敢言⑦?"阿兄得闻之,怅然心中烦。举言谓阿妹:"作计何不量⑧!先嫁得府吏,后嫁得郎君,否泰如天地⑨,足以荣汝身。不嫁义郎体,其往欲何云⑩?"兰芝仰头答:"理实如兄言。谢家事夫婿,中道还兄门,处分适兄意⑪,那得自任专?虽与府吏要⑫,渠会永无缘⑬!登即相许和⑭,便可作婚姻。"

A worthy, excellent and handsome youth,
Himself aspired to wed the fair Lanzhi.
So to the brother's house they came once more,
This time as envoys from the Prefect sent.
The flowery, official greetings o'er,
They told the special reason they had come.
The mother, torn this way and that, declared:
"My child has vowed she ne'er will wed again.
I fear I know no way to change her mind."
But Lanzhi's brother, ever worldly-wise,
Was never slow to seize a heaven-sent chance,
And to his sister spoke blunt words and harsh:
"See you not, girl, how much this profits you?
Your former husband held a petty post.
Now comes an offer from the Prefect's son:
A greater contrast would be hard to find.
Turn down this offer if you will, this prize,
But think not I shall find you daily rice!"
What must be, must be, then thought poor Lanzhi
"Brother," she said, "what you have said is good.
I was a wife and now am none again;
I left you once and then came back again
To dwell beneath your hospitable roof.
Your will is such as cannot be gainsaid.
True, to Zhongqing I gave my plighted word,
Yet faint the hope of seeing him again!
Your counsel I must welcome as a boon:
Pray you, arrange the ceremony soon."

①诺诺：表示同意的答应声。尔尔：犹言就这样，就这样。

②部：这里指太守府。

③大有缘：指话语十分投机。

④历、书：都指历书。这句是说反复查阅历书，选择结婚吉日。

⑤六合：古人把农历每月所置之辰称为月建，如正月建寅，二月建卯等，用干支纪日叫日辰。选择良辰吉日，需月建与日辰相合，即子与丑合，寅与亥合，卯与戌合，辰与酉合，巳与申合，午与未合，称六合。合是吉日，不合叫冲，不是吉日。相应：相合。

⑥良吉：良辰吉日。

⑦成婚：指洽谈筹办婚事。

⑧交语：交相传话。速装束：赶快筹措结婚用品。

⑨浮云：比喻人多。

⑩鹄(hú 狐)：鸟名，即天鹅。

⑪幡(fān 帆)：一种旗子。

⑫婀(ē 屙)娜(nuó 挪)：轻盈柔美貌。

⑬踯(zhí 直)躅(zhú 竹)：指缓步行进。青骢(cōng 聪)马：青白色相杂的马。

⑭流苏：垂在马鞍下做装饰的穗子。金镂(lòu 漏)鞍：以金属雕花为装饰的马鞍。

⑮赍(jī 鸡)：付给，送给。赍钱：指聘礼。

⑯杂彩：指各色的丝织品。

⑰交：交州，今广东、广西大部和越南一部分。广：广州，三国时

媒人下床去，诺诺复尔尔①。还部白府君②："下官奉使命，言谈大有缘③。"府君得闻之，心中大欢喜。视历复开书④，便利此月内，六合正相应⑤。"良吉三十日⑥，今已二十七，卿可去成婚⑦。"交语速装束⑧，络绎如浮云⑨。青雀白鹄舫⑩，四角龙子幡⑪，婀娜随风转⑫；金车玉作轮，踯躅青骢马⑬，流苏金镂鞍⑭。赍钱三百万⑮，皆用青丝穿。杂彩三百匹⑯，交、广市鲑珍⑰。从人四五百，郁郁登郡门⑱。

吴分交州一部分为广州。市：买。鲑(xié 鞋)珍：泛指珍贵的菜肴。

⑱郁郁：盛多貌。登郡门：会集在太守衙门。

When he heard this, the official go-between
Agreed to everything the brother asked.
Then to the Prefect's house they hurried back
To tell the happy outcome of their work.
It seemed so good a marriage for his son,
The Prefect thought, that full of sheer delight
He turned the pages of the almanac,
And therein found the most auspicious date
To be the thirtieth of that same month.
Whereon he summoned his subordinates:
"The thirtieth is a heaven-favoured day,"
Said he, "and that is but three days away.
Have all in readiness to greet the bride."
The household was abuzz from floor to roof
As was befitting for a noble match.
There were, to fetch the bride, gay gondolas
Fresh-painted with designs of lucky birds
And silken pennants fluttering o'er the deck.
There were gold carriages with jade inlay
And well-groomed horses of the finest breed
With saddles shining, harness all arrayed!
As for the presents, strings of cash they told
Three thousand, bolts of silk and brocade
Three hundred. And among those precious gifts
Were globe-fish brought from some far distant clime.
The welcoming cortege, five hundred strong,
Would gladden all eyes as it passed along.

阿母谓阿女:"适得府君书①,明日来迎汝。何不作衣裳?莫令事不举②!"阿女默无声,手巾掩口啼,泪落便如泻。移我琉璃榻③,出置前窗下。左手持刀尺,右手执绫罗,朝成绣袷裙,晚成单罗衫。晻晻日欲暝④,愁思出门啼。

①适:刚才。

②莫令:不要使。事不举:事情办不成。

③榻:一种坐具,比床短。琉璃:一种矿石质的有色半透明体材料。琉璃榻是指镶嵌有琉璃的榻。

④晻(yǎn 掩)晻:日光渐暗。暝(míng 名):日落,日暮。

64

In the bride's house the troubled mother said:
"Lanzhi, the Prefect's messengers have come.
The welcoming party will arrive full soon.
'Tis time you donned your bridal finery.
You have agreed... No time to tarry now!"
Lanzhi, too sad to utter any word,
Sobbed neath her kerchief to conceal her grief,
Her pale, pale cheeks all wet with bitter tears.
She dragged a chair with heavy marble seat
Towards the window where there was more light,
Took silk and scissors, measure, needle, braid,
Cut out in grief and wet her thread with tears.
Ere noon a jacket new and skirt she made;
By eve a wedding gown was all complete.
Then in the twilight, desperate, forlorn,
Out at the gate she stole to weep alone.

Then, suddenly, her sobbing died away...
Far off she heard a horse's anguished neigh!
Oh, that familiar neigh! Yet why so sore?
Indeed Zhongqing was riding fast that way.
The master had heard news, lost heart, asked leave.
The very steed, too, his forebodings shared.
At last, her straining eyes perceived him clear:
His presence filled her with both joy and pain.

①此变:指兰芝答应再嫁的事。

②求假:请假。

③摧藏:当是凄怆的假借字。

④蹑履:缓步行走。

⑤使心伤:使人伤心。

⑥父母、弟兄:指母、兄。

⑦还:还家。

⑧高迁:高升,指兰芝再嫁太守之子。

⑨卒:终,直至。

⑩旦夕间:朝夕之间,言时间之短。

⑪日胜贵:一天天高贵。

⑫不复全:不能再保全生命了。

　　府吏闻此变①,因求假暂归②。未至二三里,摧藏马悲哀③。新妇识马声,蹑履相逢迎④,怅然遥相望,知是故人来。举手拍马鞍,嗟叹使心伤⑤。"自君别我后,人事不可量,果不如先愿,又非君所详。我有亲父母,逼迫兼弟兄⑥,以我应他人,君还何所望⑦!"府吏谓新妇:"贺卿得高迁⑧!磐石方且厚,可以卒千年⑨;蒲苇一时纫,便作旦夕间⑩。卿当日胜贵⑪,吾独向黄泉。"新妇谓府吏:"何意出此言!同是被逼迫,君尔妾亦然。黄泉下相见,勿违今日言!"执手分道去,各各还家门。生人作死别,恨恨那可论!念与世间辞,千万不复全⑫。

Patting the horse, she heaved a woeful sigh.
"Zhongqing, my darling, at our parting dire
None could foresee the course events would take.
You cannot guess my abject misery,
But all we hoped is now an empty dream.
My mother you knew well. My tyrant brother,
'Twas he who schemed to wed me to another.
Now that the die is cast by fate austere,
What more can you expect of me, my dear?"
Zhongqing, heart-stricken, forced himself to say,
"May you know every happiness, Lanzhi!
The rock stands fixed, unyielding evermore,
But oh! I fear the fibres of the vine
Have lost their toughness all too easily...
May you be rich and live in happy state,
But as for me, why, death shall be my fate!"
That stung her to the quick, but she replied,
"Why say such cruel things to me, my dear?
We both are shipwrecked on the sea of life,
Our vessels foundered by the ruthless gale.
Life has enjoined that man and wife must sever:
Let us both die, and be one flesh for ever!"
Long hand in hand they stayed before they went
With mournful steps and slow their different ways —
Two lovers, parting, knowing all too well
That death alone could make them one again.
All roads to joy fast blocked, they did not quail,
But vowed to terminate their tragic tale.

①严霜:浓霜,寒霜。结:冻结。庭兰:庭院中的兰花。

②日冥冥:日暮。比喻自己不久于世。

③令:使。在后单:意指自己死后,母亲孤单一人。

④不良计:不好的打算,指自杀。

⑤四体:四肢,指身体。康且直:身体健康而舒适。

⑥大家子:出身门第高贵的人。台阁:指尚书台。

⑦贵贱:焦母认为仲卿出身高贵而兰芝则出身低贱。情何薄:因贵贱不同,焦家遗弃兰芝谈不上是薄情。

⑧艳城郭:犹云全城数她最艳丽。

⑨复:指求婚的回音。

⑩作计:指打算自杀的主意。乃尔:如此。立:确定。

⑪愁煎迫:被忧愁煎熬压迫。以上二句是说仲卿打定主意之后,转头向门里看到老母,心里又非常忧愁痛苦。

府吏还家去,上堂拜阿母:"今日大风寒,寒风摧树木,严霜结庭兰①。儿今日冥冥②,令母在后单③。故作不良计④,勿复怨鬼神!命如南山石,四体康且直⑤。"阿母得闻之,零泪应声落。"汝是大家子,仕宦于台阁⑥。慎勿为妇死,贵贱情何薄⑦?东家有贤女,窈窕艳城郭⑧。阿母为汝求,便复在旦夕⑨。"府吏再拜还,长叹空房中,作计乃尔立⑩。转头向户里,渐见愁煎迫⑪。

When Zhongqing, heavy-hearted, reached his home,
Straight to his mother's room he went, and bowed.
"The weather changes, mother. Bitter cold,
A terrifying wind sears leaf and tree.
The frost congeals the orchids, all the flowers,
And Zhongqing's life, too, draws unto its close.
His sole regret is leaving you alone,
But 'tis his own desire to end life so —
No ghost, no devil, mother, holds him thrall!
Your son is like the rocks of Nanshan Range,
Immutable in death, immune to change."
The mother heard these words in sore amaze,
But guessed their cause, and pitied him in tears.
"My son, sole heir of noble family,
What great and glorious prospects lie ahead!
Why for a wanton should you think to die,
One so inferior in every way?
As I have told you, in the neighbourhood
There dwells a paragon of loveliness.
Soon will I send a go-between to her,
And long and happy years be yours, my son!"
But he kept silence, bowed right low, and left,
Long, long his empty room he paced, and thought
A myriad thoughts of Lanzhi, love, and death.
Oft glanced he sadly towards his mother's room;
The world seemed shrouded in a pall of gloom!

其日牛马嘶①，新妇入青庐②。庵庵黄昏后③，寂寂人定初④。"我命绝今日，魂去尸长留。"揽裙脱丝履⑤，举身赴清池⑥。府吏闻此事，心知长别离。徘徊庭树下，自挂东南枝⑦。

①牛马嘶：指迎亲的牛马嘶鸣。

②青庐：青布围搭成的帏帐。

③庵庵：通晻，日光渐暗。

④人初定：指夜深人定之时。

⑤揽裙：撩起裙子。

⑥举身：犹言纵身。

⑦自挂：指自缢。

The day for Lanzhi's splendid wedding came,
She lonelier than ever mid the throng.
She waited, waited till the night should fall.
At last the turmoil ceased, the guests thinned out.
"This is the day," she mused, "My journey's end.
My soul will wander, though my corpse remain."
The pond's dark waters beckoned, cold and chill.
Barefoot she waded in, and all was still.
Though for the news Zhongqing was half-prepared,
It nowise lighter made the dreadful blow.
Beneath the courtyard trees release he sought,
He turned southeast, and then the rope went taut...

两家求合葬,合葬华山傍①。东西植松柏,左右种梧桐,枝枝相覆盖,叶叶相交通②。中有双飞鸟,自名为鸳鸯,仰头相向鸣③,夜夜达五更。行人驻足听④,寡妇起彷徨。多谢后世人⑤,戒之慎勿忘⑥。

①华山:当地的一个山名。

②交通:指树叶相连接。

③相向:相对。

④驻足:停下脚步。

⑤谢:告,告诉。

⑥戒之:以上面这件事为教训。

Linked in a common grief, the families
Buried the lovers beside Mount Huashan.
And all around the graveyard grow dark pines,
Through all the changing seasons ever green,
With cypress interspersed and parasol trees.
Like loving arms the branches intertwine,
And lovingly the leaves and sprays caress;
And in the foliage dwell two little birds,
That mate for life, whose very name is love.
They cross their bills and sing to one another
Their soft endearments all night long till dawn,
And passersby stand spell-bound at the sound,
And lonely widows wake to hear and muse
Upon this story of a bygone day
Which shall endure till all shall pass away.

《古诗十九首》代表了汉代文人五言诗的最高成就,被称为"五言之冠冕"。其内容多不离思妇、游子,长于抒情。本篇既以孤竹结根于泰山起兴,又以兔丝附于女萝为比,再托物喻意,借伤草木凋零,发美人迟暮之感叹。

冉冉孤生竹①,结根泰山阿②。
与君为新婚③,菟丝附女萝④。
菟丝生有时,夫妇会有宜⑤。
千里远结婚,悠悠隔山陂⑥。
思君令人老,轩车来何迟⑦?
伤彼蕙兰花⑧,含英扬光辉⑨;
过时而不采,将随秋草萎。
君亮执高节⑩,贱妾亦何为⑪?

①冉冉:柔弱貌。

②泰山:同太山,大山。阿:山坳。

③为新婚:指订婚。

④菟丝:一种旋花科的蔓生植物,女子自比。 女萝:一说即"松萝",一种缘松而生的蔓生植物,以比女子的丈夫。

⑤宜:适当的时间。这两句是说,菟丝及时而生,夫妇亦当及时相会。

⑥陂(bēi 杯):池塘,水泽。

⑦轩车:此指迎娶的蓬车。

⑧蕙、兰:两种同类香草,女子自比。

⑨含英扬光辉:花含苞待放。

⑩亮:同"谅",料想。

⑪这两句是说,君想必守志不渝,我又何苦自艾自怨。

Soft and pliant, the lonely bamboo
Rooted in the mountain;
But, married to you,
I am like the dodder clinging to a vine.
As the dodder has its season of growth,
So husband and wife should have time to be together,
Yet a thousand *li* divide us since we married,
Far-stretching mountain ranges lie between.
Longing for you makes me old before my time,
It seems your covered carriage will never come!
I grieve for the orchid,
So splendid when it flowers,
For unless plucked in time
It will only wither away like the grass in autumn.
What can I do
But trust in your constancy?

这首诗是古代文学作品中最早借牛郎、织女星的传说抒写爱情的作品，具有浓郁的浪漫主义色彩，与秦观的"纤云弄巧，飞星传恨，银汉迢迢暗度……"(《鹊桥仙》)对比读来，更别有一番情趣。

迢迢牵牛星①，皎皎河汉女②。
纤纤擢素手③，札札弄机杼④；
终日不成章⑤，泣涕零如雨⑥；
河汉清且浅，相去复几许⑦！
盈盈一水间⑧，脉脉不得语⑨。

①迢迢：远貌。牵牛星：即民间所称牛郎星。

②皎皎：明貌。河汉：即银河。河汉女，指织女星。

③擢：举，摆动。素手：白手。

④札札：机织声。

⑤终日不成章：说织女终日也织不成布。章：指布匹上的经纬纹理。

⑥零：落。

⑦几许：犹言"几何"。

⑧盈盈：水清浅貌。间：隔。

⑨脉脉：含情相视貌。

76

Far, far away, the Cowherd,
Fair, fair, the Weaving Maid; ①
Nimbly move her slender white fingers,
Click-clack goes her weaving-loom.
All day she weaves, yet her web is still not done
And her tears fall like rain.
Clear and shallow the Milky Way,
They are not far apart!
But the stream brims always between
And, gazing at each other, they cannot speak.

---

① The Cowherd and the Weaving Maid are the Chinese names for two constellations separated by the Milky Way.

曹操开建安文学风气之先,而《短歌行》是一首"言志诗"。诗中通篇比兴,引用了《诗经》成句,不仅毫不晦涩,反而更显其立意之深远、气韵之沉雄、诗情之跌宕,体现了"志深笔长,梗概多气"的建安风骨。

①对酒当歌:面对着酒和歌。当:与"对"义近,都是面对的意思。

②朝露:早晨的露水。

③慨当以慷:犹言既慷且慨。慷慨是意气激昂的意思。

④幽思:深藏着的心事,即"忧世不治"。

⑤杜康:相传是我国最早发明酿酒的人,这里用以代指酒。

⑥青衿:周朝时学子的服装,用在诗里代指学子,这里指有智谋、有才干的人。衿:衣领。

⑦悠悠:形容思念的深沉和久长。

⑧沉吟:低声吟咏,指深切怀念和吟味的样子。

⑨苹:艾蒿。

⑩鼓:弹奏。

⑪掇(duō):拾取。一说掇同辍(chuò 绰),停止,断绝。

对酒当歌①,人生几何?
譬如朝露②,去日苦多。
慨当以慷③,幽思难忘④。
何以解忧?唯有杜康⑤。
青青子衿⑥,悠悠我心⑦。
但为君故,沉吟至今⑧。
呦呦鹿鸣,食野之苹⑨。
我有嘉宾,鼓瑟吹笙⑩。
明明如月,何时可掇⑪?
忧从中来,不可断绝。
越陌度阡,枉用相存。
契阔谈䜩,心念旧恩。
月明星稀,乌鹊南飞,
绕树三匝,何枝可依?
山不厌高,海不厌深。
周公吐哺,天下归心。

Wine before us, sing a song.
How long does life last?
It is like the morning dew;
Sad so many days have past.

Sing hey, sing ho!
Deep within my heart I pine.
Nothing can dispel my woe,
Save Du Kang, the god of wine.

Blue, blue the scholar's robe;
Long, long for him I ache.
Preoccupied with you, my lord,
Heavy thoughts for your sake.

To each other cry the deer,
Nibbling grass upon the plain.
When a good friend visits me,
We'll play the lyre once again.

In the sky, the moon is bright;
Yet I can reach it never.
In my heart such sorrow dwells;
Remaining with me ever.

①阡、陌:田间小路,南北为
阡,东西为陌。

②枉:枉驾,屈驾。用:以。
存:存问。这句是说,劳驾贤士
来相存问。

③契阔:聚合和分散,这里
有久别重逢之意。谈:谈心。
讌:同宴。这句是说,久别重逢,
我当推心置腹地与之交谈,设宴
招待。

④旧恩:旧日的友好情谊。

⑤匝(zā 扎):周。

⑥厌:满足。

⑦吐哺:吐出口中正在咀嚼
的食物,指中途停止吃饭。《韩
诗外传》卷三记载周公曾说:
"吾,文王之子,武王之弟,成王
之叔父也,又相天下,吾于天下
亦不轻矣。然一沐三握发,一饭
三吐哺,犹恐失天下之士。"这里
曹操显然是以周公自命的。

对酒当歌,人生几何?
譬如朝露,去日苦多。
慨当以慷,幽思难忘。
何以解忧? 唯有杜康。
青青子衿,悠悠我心。
但为君故,沉吟至今。
呦呦鹿鸣,食野之苹。
我有嘉宾,鼓瑟吹笙。
明明如月,何时可掇?
忧从中来,不可断绝。
越陌度阡①,枉用相存②。
契阔谈讌③,心念旧恩④。
月明星稀,乌鹊南飞,
绕树三匝⑤,何枝可依?
山不厌高,海不厌深⑥。
周公吐哺⑦,天下归心。

In the fields, our paths crossed;
Your visit was so kind.
Together after our long parting,
Your favours come to mind.

Bright the moon, few the stars;
The crows in southward flight.
Circling three times round the tree,
No branch where to alight.

What if the mountain is high,
Or how deep the sea?
When the Duke of Zhou greeted a guest,
In his service all wished to be.

汉代文人诗歌至建安时期以"三曹"、"七子"和蔡琰为代表,形成了慷慨悲壮的独特风格,人称"建安风骨"。《观沧海》是诗史上最早的一首完整的山水诗,以雄健的笔调,开阔的胸襟,写壮阔的沧海景色,抒英雄暮年之愁、建功立业之志,"有吞吐宇宙气象"(沈德潜《古诗源》)。

东临碣石①,以观沧海。
水何澹澹②,山岛竦峙③。
树木丛生,百草丰茂。
秋风萧瑟④,洪波涌起。
日月之行,若出其中;
星汉灿烂⑤,若出其里。
幸甚至哉,歌以咏志⑥。

①碣石:山名,在今河北省乐亭县西南。也有说当时的碣石山今已沉陷海中。

②何:多么。澹澹:浩荡平满的样子。

③山岛:指碣石山,当时的碣石山在海边上。竦(sǒng 竦)峙(zhì 至):高峻挺拔的样子。

④萧瑟:秋风声。

⑤星汉:天河。

⑥"幸甚"二句:是乐工合乐时加上去的,并无实际意思。

Come east of Jieshi Cliff①
I gaze out across the ocean,
Its rolling waves
Studded with rocks and islets;
Dense the trees and bushes here,
Rank the undergrowth;
The autumn wind is soughing,
Huge billows are breaking.
Sun and moon take their course
As if risen from the sea;
The bright galaxy of stars
Seems sprung from the deep.
And so, with joy in my heart,
I hum this song.

① This cliff southwest of Leting County in Hebei Province has now been submerged by the sea.

本诗是以诗喻理的佳作。建安诗人常发人生短促、荣辱难以把握的忧思，而能以豪迈、昂扬的精神，唱出"老骥伏枥，志在千里；烈士暮年，壮心不已"这般志士胸怀的，则非雄才大略的曹孟德莫属！

神龟虽寿①，犹有竟时②。
腾蛇乘雾③，终为土灰。
老骥伏枥④，志在千里；
烈士暮年⑤，壮心不已。
盈缩之期⑥，不但在天；
养怡之福⑦，可得永年⑧。
幸甚至哉，歌以咏志。

①神龟：传说中的一种长寿龟。

②竟：终极，终了。

③腾蛇：传说中的一种能驾雾飞行的蛇。

④骥：千里马。枥，马槽。骥因年老体衰，故伏于槽中。

⑤烈士：重义轻生，有志建功立业的人。

⑥盈缩之期：指人的寿命长短。

⑦养：保养。怡：愉快。

⑧永年：长寿。

Though the tortoise blessed with magic powers lives long,
Its days have their allotted span;
Though winged serpents ride high on the mist,
They turn to dust and ashes at the last;
An old war-horse may be stabled,
Yet still it longs to gallop a thousand *li* ;
And a noble-hearted man though advanced in years
Never abandons his proud aspirations.
Man's span of life, whether long or short,
Depends not on Heaven alone;
One who eats well and keeps cheerful
Can live to a great old age.
And so, with joy in my heart,
I hum this song.

本诗真实、深刻地反映了汉末的社会动荡和人民的苦难,推动了文人诗现实主义传统的发扬,被人视作杜甫《无家别》、《垂老别》诸篇之祖。其中名句"出门无所见,白骨蔽平原",与曹操的"白骨露于野,千里无鸡鸣"(《蒿里行》)异曲同工。

西京乱无象①,豺虎方遘患②。
复弃中国去③,委身适荆蛮④。
亲戚对我悲,朋友相追攀⑤。
出门无所见,白骨蔽平原。
路有饥妇人,抱子弃草间。
顾闻号泣声,挥涕独不还:
"未知身死处,何能两相完⑥?"
驱马弃之去,不忍听此言。
南登霸陵岸⑦,回首望长安。
悟彼下泉人⑧,喟然伤心肝⑨。

①西京:指长安,西汉时的国都。无象:无章法,无传统。

②豺虎:指东汉末董卓的部将李傕、郭汜等。遘:同构。遘患:这里指给人民造成灾难。

③中国:中原地区。

④委身:置身。适:往。荆蛮:即指荆州。

⑤追攀:追逐攀车,表示依依不舍的样子。

⑥完:保全。

⑦霸陵:汉文帝刘恒的陵墓,在今陕西省长安县东。

⑧悟:领悟,懂得。《下泉》为《诗经·曹风》中的一个篇名,汉代经师们认为这是一首曹国人怀念明王贤伯的诗。下泉人:《下泉》诗的作者。

⑨喟(kuì愧)然:伤心的样子。

The Western Capital is in turmoil,
Jackals and tigers are running riot.
Once again I leave the Central Plains,
Going to seek refuge in barbarous Jing.
My kindred look at me in deep grief,
Friends see me off, reluctant to part.
Out of the gate a bleak view meets my eye;
The plain is strewn with white bones.
On the road I see a starving woman,
Who abandons her child in the grass.
Turning round, she hears the wailing.
She wipes her tears and goes on alone.
"I don't know where I myself shall die,
How can I look after both of us?"
Driving my horse on, I leave her behind,
For I cannot bear to hear such sad words.
To the south I climb the mound of Baling,
Turning my head, I gaze at the capital.
The theme of "Downward Spring"① dawns on me,
I sigh, my heart tortured with agony.

---

① A poem, in the *Book of Songs*, which expresses people's nostalgia for the sage kings and their powerful and prosperous reigns in the past.

曹植是建安诗人中最注重艺术表现力的一位。建安诗歌脱胎于汉乐府，至曹植而成为典型的文人诗。《美女篇》以美女未得佳偶而不嫁，比喻志士未遇明主，不能施展抱负。写法上模仿《陌上桑》，但其词采之华茂绚丽，却与汉乐府《陌上桑》迥异。

①美女：以比君子。用"美人"、"美女"比喻君子，是屈原以来文人诗赋中常用的手法。妖且闲：艳丽而且文静。

②冉冉：轻轻摇动的样子。

③攘(rǎng 嚷)袖：卷袖。

④约金环：戴着金制的手镯。约，围，套着。

⑤金爵钗：一端饰有雀形的金钗。爵，同雀。

⑥翠：墨绿色。 琅(láng 郎)玕(gān 干)：一种似玉的美石。

⑦交：佩带。

⑧间：夹杂。木难：珠名。

⑨裾(jū 居)：衣襟。 还(xuán 旋)：通旋，摆动的样子。

⑩遗：流动。

⑪用：因。息驾：停车。休者：指在路边休息的人。

美女妖且闲①，采桑歧路间。
柔条纷冉冉②，叶落何翩翩！
攘袖见素手③，皓腕约金环④。
头上金爵钗⑤，腰佩翠琅玕⑥。
明珠交玉体⑦，珊瑚间木难⑧。
罗衣何飘飘，轻裾随风还⑨。
顾盼遗光彩⑩，长啸气若兰。
行徒用息驾，休者以忘餐⑪。
借问女安居？乃在城南端。
青楼临大路，高门结重关。
容华耀朝日，谁不希令颜，
媒氏何所营？玉帛不时安。
佳人慕高义，求贤良独难。
众人徒嗷嗷，安知彼所观。
盛年处房室，中夜起长叹。

Alluring and shy, stands a fair maiden,
Gathering mulberry leaves at the crossroads.
The tender twigs rustle;
The leaves fall one by one.
How white her hands as she bares her arms,
A gold bracelet round her wrist!
On her head a golden sparrow hairpin;
At her waist a green jade pendant,
While encompassing her lovely form,
Pearls, coral and blue glass beads.
In the breeze, her silk blouse flutters
And her light skirt flows.
Glances reveal her shining eyes;
Sighs her breath, orchid sweet.
Travellers en route halt their carriages;
Those resting forget their refreshment.
If someone asks where she lives,
Her home is in the south of the city.

①青楼:以青漆为饰的楼,是
富贵之家的闺阁。宋元以后始用
青楼代指娼家。

②重关:两道门栓,极言门户
之严紧。

③容华:容颜。

④希:仰望。令:美。

⑤媒氏:媒人。营:经营,做事
情。

⑥玉帛:珪璋和束素。这里即
泛指定婚的彩礼。不时安:不及时
安置。以上两句是说,对于这么好
的女子,媒人们都干什么了,为什
么订婚的彩礼还没有人及时地来
下?

⑦观:着眼点,指标准、条件。
以上四句是说,美人所敬慕的是有
崇高道德和远大理想的人,而这样
的贤良之士是实在难找的。一般
人光知道嗷嗷乱叫,谁能知道美人
自己的着眼点是什么呢?

⑧盛年:正当年,含义是已经
不小了。处房室:指未出嫁。古代
称未嫁女子曰"处女"、"室女"。以
上二句是用美女已到年龄而仍未
出嫁,半夜不眠徘徊叹息,以比喻
诗人的有抱负而不能施展之情。

美女妖且闲,采桑歧路间。
柔条纷冉冉,叶落何翩翩!
攘袖见素手,皓腕约金环。
头上金爵钗,腰佩翠琅玕。
明珠交玉体,珊瑚间木难。
罗衣何飘飘,轻裾随风还。
顾盼遗光彩,长啸气若兰。
行徒用息驾,休者以忘餐。
借问女安居?乃在城南端。
青楼临大路①,高门结重关②。
容华耀朝日③,谁不希令颜④,
媒氏何所营⑤?玉帛不时安⑥。
佳人慕高义,求贤良独难。
众人徒嗷嗷,安知彼所观⑦。
盛年处房室⑧,中夜起长叹。

A green, storied house by the highway,
With a high gate and double bars.
Radiant as the morning sun,
Who could not admire her beauty?
Why aren't the matchmakers busy?
Where are the silk and jade betrothal gifts?
This fair maiden longs for a worthy lover;
Yet how hard to find a fitting mate.
In vain people make suggestions,
Ignorant of her ideal.
Wasting her youth away in her home,
At midnight she awakes and sighs.

归园田居(其一)·陶渊明(365—427)

东晋玄言诗风占据文坛统治地位,"理过其辞,淡乎寡味"。陶渊明开创了田园诗一体,以平淡自然的笔调,勾画田园风光,抒写乡村生活的恬静心境,被称作"陶体"。标志着古典诗歌从题材到风格的突破,孕育了盛唐田园山水诗派,为古典诗歌开辟出新的境界。

少无适俗韵①,性本爱丘山。
误落尘网中②,一去三十年③。
羁鸟恋旧林,池鱼思故渊。
开荒南野际④,守拙归园田⑤。
方宅十余亩⑥,草屋八九间。
榆柳荫后檐,桃李罗堂前⑦。
暧暧远人村⑧,依依墟里烟⑨。
狗吠深巷中,鸡鸣桑树颠。
户庭无尘杂,虚室有余闲⑩。
久在樊笼里,复得返自然。

①适俗:适应世俗。韵:情调、风度。

②尘网:指尘世,官府生活污浊而又拘束,犹如网罗。这里指仕途。

③三十年:当作"十三年"。陶渊明自太元十八年(393)初仕为江州祭酒,到义熙元年(405)辞彭泽令归田,恰好是十三个年头。

④际:间。

⑤守拙:守正不阿。

⑥方:旁。这句是说住宅周围有土地十余亩。

⑦罗:罗列。

⑧暧(ài 爱)暧:暗淡的样子。

⑨墟里:村落。

⑩虚室:闲静的屋子。

From youth I was never made for common life,
My nature was ever to love the hills and mountains.
By mischance I fell into the dusty world
And, being gone, stayed there for thirteen years.
A captive bird longs for the woods of old,
The fish in the pond dreams of its native river.
So I have returned to till this southern wild,
To a simple life in my own fields and garden.
Two acres of land surround my home,
My thatched cottage has eight or nine bays,
Willow and elm shade the courtyard,
Peach and plum spread in front of the hall.
Dim, dim in the distance lies the village,
Faintly, faintly you see the smoke of its chimneys.
A dog barks deep in the long lane,
The cock crows on the top of a mulberry tree.
There is no dust and no confusion here,
In these empty rooms, but ample space to spare.
So long have I lived inside a cage!
Now at last I can turn again to Nature.

饮酒(其五)·陶渊明(365—427)

陶潜在这首田园诗中,将田园之乐、隐居之乐、悟道之乐融为一体,于平淡自然之中揭示深刻的人生哲理。"采菊东篱下,悠然见南山。山气日夕佳,飞鸟相与还。"为千古名句。全诗营构意境之深远,正是王国维所谓的"无我之境,不知何者为我,何者为物"(《人间词话》)。

结庐在人境,而无车马喧①。
问君何能尔? 心远地自偏②。
采菊东篱下,悠然见南山③。
山气日夕佳,飞鸟相与还④。
此中有真意,欲辨已忘言。

①结庐:构筑屋子。人境:人间,人类居住的地方。
②君:作者自谓。尔:如此、这样。
③南山:指庐山。
④日夕:傍晚。相与:相交,结伴。

I have built my cottage amongst the throng of men,
And yet there is no noise of horse and of carriage.
You ask me, how can it be? and I reply:
When my heart is absent the place itself is absent;
For I pick chrysanthemums under the eastern hedge,
And far away to the south I can see the mountains,
And the mountain mists are lovely at morning and evening,
While birds keep flying across and back again.
In all these things there lies a profound meaning.
I was going to explain ... but now I forget what it was.

陶渊明以前，傅玄和陆机都写过《挽歌诗》，以虚拟手法对死亡故作达观，实则是魏晋易代以来文人惧祸心理的折射。而陶潜《挽歌诗》既有志向难伸的牢骚、激愤，又以坦荡的胸襟置生死、荣辱于度外，这才是真正的达观，是更高远的精神境界。

荒草何茫茫，白杨亦萧萧。
严霜九月中，送我出远郊。
四面无人居，高坟正嶕峣①。
马为仰天鸣，风为自萧条。
幽室一已闭，千年不复朝②。
千年不复朝，贤达无奈何③。
向来相送人，各自还其家④。
亲戚或余悲，他人亦已歌⑤。
死去何所道，托体同山阿⑥。

①嶕（jiāo 交）峣（yáo 尧）：很高的样子。

②幽室：指墓穴。这两句是说墓穴一旦被封闭，就如同黑夜，永远不会天亮了。

③这两句是说对于死，贤人达士也无可奈何。

④向：昔，刚才。

⑤或余悲：有些人仍含悲痛。亦已歌：也就歌唱快乐了。

⑥山阿：山陵。

Lonely the vast expanse of withered grass,
Whispering, sighing, the white poplar① leaves!
There's bitter frost now in this autumn month,
When they've brought me here out of the town so far.
No one lives near this place,
Only the mounds stand tall around —
A horse looks up at the sky and neighs,
The wind itself blows desolately.
When that dark room is once closed,
In a thousand years I'll never see out again,
In a thousand years, never see out again!
Virtue and wisdom are no avail whatever.
Those who have come here to see me off
Will soon return, each to his own home;
Relations perhaps will be sorry a little longer,
The others will merely finish the chant and go.
Dead and gone — there's nothing more to be said —
My body I now entrust to be mingled with the hills.

---

① Commonly grown on graveyards.

晚登三山还望京邑·谢朓(464—499)

南朝宋初的谢灵运和齐代的谢朓，都是著名山水诗人，文学史上称为大谢小谢。与大谢诗的富艳精工不同，小谢诗以清新流丽著称。本诗是谢朓山水诗的代表作，其中"余霞散成绮，澄江静如练"为历代传诵的写景名句。

"三山"位于今南京市长江南岸；"京邑"即金陵，位于今南京市东南。

灞涘望长安，河阳视京县①。
白日丽飞甍，参差皆可见②。
余霞散成绮，澄江静如练③。
喧鸟覆春洲，杂英满芳甸④。
去矣方滞淫，怀哉罢欢宴⑤。
佳期怅何许，泪下如流霰⑥。
有情知望乡，谁能鬒不变⑦！

①灞(bà 霸)涘(sì 四)：灞水岸。河阳：县名，故城在今河南孟县西。京县：指洛阳。
②飞甍(méng 萌)：飞竿的屋檐。
③绮：锦缎。练：白绸。
④甸：郊野。
⑤方：将。滞淫：淹留。怀哉：想念啊。
⑥佳期：指还乡邑之期。霰(xiàn 现)：雪粒。
⑦鬒(zhěn 诊)：黑发。

98

Like Wang Can gazing at Chang'an from the bank,
Or Pan Yue at Luoyang, north of the Yellow River,
Here I see in the distance everywhere
Tiled roofs resplendent in the sunlight.
The sky at sunset like a coloured brocade;
The river calm like a skein of white silk.
Crying waterfowl flock to the islet;
Flowers of many hues fill the fragrant meadows.
I wish to return home. Why linger here?
I long to end this merry-making.
When will the time to return come?
Till then my tears like falling rain;
So deeply for home I pine.
Can I help it if my hair turns grey?

本诗为北朝民歌的代表作,与《孔雀东南飞》并称我国古代叙事的"双璧"。明人胡应麟称赞:"五言之赡,极于焦仲卿妻;杂言之赡,极于木兰"(《诗薮》)。全诗朴素流畅,以浓郁的民歌色彩,生动地刻画出文学史上一位不朽的女英雄形象。

唧唧复唧唧①,木兰当户织。不闻机杼声②,唯闻女叹息。问女何所思?问女何所忆③?女亦无所思,女亦无所忆。昨夜见军帖④,可汗大点兵⑤,军书十二卷,卷卷有爷名⑥。阿爷无大儿,木兰无长兄,愿为市鞍马⑦,从此替爷征。

东市买骏马,西市买鞍鞯⑧,南市买辔头⑨,北市买长鞭。旦辞爷娘去⑩,暮宿黄河边。不闻爷娘唤女声,但闻黄河流水鸣溅溅⑪。旦辞黄河去,暮至黑山头,不闻爷娘唤女声,但闻燕山胡骑鸣啾啾。

万里赴戎机,关山度若飞。朔气传金柝,寒光照铁衣。将军百战死,壮士十年归。

归来见天子,天子坐明堂。策勋十二转,赏赐百千强。可汗问所欲,木兰不用尚书郎,愿驰明驼千里足,送儿还故乡。

爷娘闻女来,出郭相扶将。阿姊闻妹来,当户理红妆。小弟闻姊来,磨刀霍霍向猪羊。开我东阁门,坐我西阁床。脱我战时袍,著我旧时裳。当窗理云鬓,对镜帖花黄。出门看火伴,火伴皆惊惶。同行十二年,不知木兰是女郎。

雄兔脚扑朔,雌兔眼迷离。双兔傍地走,安能辨我是雄雌!

①唧(jī机)唧:叹息声。
②杼(zhù住):织机上的梭子。
③忆:思念。
④军帖:征兵的名册。即下文的"军书"。
⑤可(kè克)汗(hán韩):当时西北部少数民族对其君主的称呼,这里当指北朝的君主。大点兵:犹言大征兵。
⑥爷:父亲,当时北方称父为"阿爷"。
⑦市:买。鞍马:指马具和马匹。
⑧鞯(jiān尖):马鞍下的垫子。
⑨辔(pèi配)头:马嚼子和马缰绳。
⑩旦:早晨。旦,一作朝。
⑪溅(jiān尖)溅:水流的声音。

One sigh after another,
Mulan sat opposite the door weaving;
But no sound of the shuttle was heard,
Except the sighs of the girl.
When asked what she was pondering over,
When asked what she had called to mind,
Nothing special the girl was pondering over,
Nothing special the girl had called to mind.
"Last night I saw the draft dispatch,
The khan is mustering a mighty army;
The roster consists of many muster rolls,
And every roll has Father's name on it.
Father has no grown son,
Nor Mulan an elder brother;
I want to buy a saddle and a horse,
And from now on fight in place of my father."

In the eastern market she bought a fine steed,
In the western market a saddle and a pad,
In the southern market a bridle,
In the northern market a long whip.
At daybreak she bid farewell to her parents,
At sunset she bivouacked by the Yellow River;
What met her ear was no longer her parents' call,
But the gurgles and splashes of the rushing waters.

①黑山：山名，即杀虎山，在今内蒙古呼和浩特市东南。

②燕山：所指未详，一说是燕然山，即今蒙古人民共和国境内之杭爱山。一说即今河北省境内的燕山山脉。胡骑(jì 骑)：指当时北方少数民族的骑兵。啾(jiū 究)啾：这里指马鸣叫声。

③戎机：军机，这里指战争。

④关：关隘要塞。

⑤朔气：北方的寒气。金柝(tuò 唾)：古代军中夜晚打更所用之刁斗。

⑥寒光：寒冷的月光。铁衣：战士穿的铁甲战袍。

⑦明堂：古代皇帝听政、选士的地方。

⑧策勋：记功。转：古代以军功授爵，军功加一等，爵高一级，谓之一转。十二，极言爵之高，非确数。

⑨百千：极言赏赐之多。强：有余。

⑩尚书郎：官名。

⑪明驼：一种日行千里的骆驼。

⑫儿：木兰自称。

⑬郭：外城。相：互相。

唧唧复唧唧，木兰当户织。不闻机杼声，唯闻女叹息。问女何所思？问女何所忆？女亦无所思，女亦无所忆。昨夜见军帖，可汗大点兵，军书十二卷，卷卷有爷名。阿爷无大儿，木兰无长兄，愿为市鞍马，从此替爷征。

东市买骏马，西市买鞍鞯，南市买辔头，北市买长鞭。旦辞爷娘去，暮宿黄河边。不闻爷娘唤女声，但闻黄河流水鸣溅溅。旦辞黄河去，暮至黑山头①，不闻爷娘唤女声，但闻燕山胡骑鸣啾啾②。

万里赴戎机③，关山度若飞④。朔气传金柝⑤，寒光照铁衣⑥。将军百战死，壮士十年归。

归来见天子，天子坐明堂⑦。策勋十二转⑧，赏赐百千强⑨。可汗问所欲，木兰不用尚书郎⑩，愿驰明驼千里足⑪，送儿还故乡⑫。

爷娘闻女来，出郭相扶将⑬。阿姊闻妹来，当户理红妆。小弟闻姊来，磨刀霍霍向猪羊。开我东阁门，坐我西阁床。脱我战时袍，著我旧时裳。当窗理云鬓，对镜帖花黄。出门看火伴，火伴皆惊惶。同行十二年，不知木兰是女郎。

雄兔脚扑朔，雌兔眼迷离。双兔傍地走，安能辨我是雄雌！

At daybreak she left the Yellow River,
At sunset she arrived at the top of the Black Hill;
What met her ear was no longer her parents' call,
But the Hu horses neighing in the Yanshan Mountains.

On the expedition of thousands of miles to the war,
She dashed across mountains and passes as if in flight;
In the chilly northern air night watches clanged,
In the frosty moonlight armour glistened.
Generals laid down their lives in a hundred battles,
And valiant soldiers returned after ten years' service.

When she returned to an audience with the Son of Heaven,
The Son of Heaven sat in the Hall of Brightness.
A promotion of many ranks was granted her for her merits,
With a reward that amounted to thousands of strings of cash.
The khan asked Mulan what she desired to do,
"I don't need any high official position,
Please lend me a sturdy camel that is fleet of foot,
And send me back to my hometown."

When her parents heard their daughter was coming,
They walked out of the town, each helping the other;
When her elder sister heard the younger sister was coming,
She decked herself out in her best by the door;
When her younger brother heard his elder sister was coming,
He whetted a knife and aimed it at a pig and a sheep.

①阁：古时女子卧房也称阁。下句"西阁"一作"西间"。

②著(zhuó卓)：穿。

③帖：同贴。六朝时，妇女流行一种装饰，即用金黄色纸，剪成星、月、花的形状，贴在额上，或在额上涂上黄色，叫贴花黄。

④火伴：伙伴。古代军人十人为一火，同一灶火吃饭，谓之同火者。

⑤扑朔：四脚爬搔的样子。

⑥迷离：眼睛眯起的样子。兔难分雌雄，俗常提起兔耳，让兔悬空，雄兔脚爬搔，为扑朔，雌兔则眯起双眼，为迷离。

⑦傍地走：贴地奔跑。

⑧安能：怎么能够。

唧唧复唧唧，木兰当户织。不闻机杼声，唯闻女叹息。问女何所思？问女何所忆？女亦无所思，女亦无所忆。昨夜见军帖，可汗大点兵，军书十二卷，卷卷有爷名。阿爷无大儿，木兰无长兄，愿为市鞍马，从此替爷征。

东市买骏马，西市买鞍鞯，南市买辔头，北市买长鞭。旦辞爷娘去，暮宿黄河边。不闻爷娘唤女声，但闻黄河流水鸣溅溅。旦辞黄河去，暮至黑山头，不闻爷娘唤女声，但闻燕山胡骑鸣啾啾。

万里赴戎机，关山度若飞。朔气传金柝，寒光照铁衣。将军百战死，壮士十年归。

归来见天子，天子坐明堂。策勋十二转，赏赐百千强。可汗问所欲，木兰不用尚书郎，愿驰明驼千里足，送儿还故乡。

爷娘闻女来，出郭相扶将。阿姊闻妹来，当户理红妆。小弟闻姊来，磨刀霍霍向猪羊。开我东阁门①，坐我西阁床。脱我战时袍，著我旧时裳②。当窗理云鬓，对镜帖花黄③。出门看火伴④，火伴皆惊惶。同行十二年，不知木兰是女郎。

雄兔脚扑朔⑤，雌兔眼迷离⑥。双兔傍地走⑦，安能辨我是雄雌⑧！

"I opened the door of my east chamber,
And then sat down on the bed in my west chamber;
Taking off the armour worn in wartime,
I attired myself in my apparel of former times;
By the window I combed and coiffed my cloudy hair,
Before the mirror I adorned my forehead with a yellow pattern."①
When she came out to meet her battle companions,
They were all astounded and thrown into bewilderment.
Together they had been in the army for a dozen years or so,
Yet none had ever known that Mulan was actually a girl.

The male rabbit kicks its fluffy feet as it scampers,
The eyes of the female rabbit are blurred by fluffy tufts of hair,
But when they run side by side in the field,
You can hardly tell the doe from the buck!

---

① It was the fashion among women at the time to decorate their foreheads with a yellow pattern in the shape of star, moon, flower or bird.

初唐诗人王勃、杨炯、卢照邻、骆宾王以文词齐名,并称"初唐四杰",其诗作在风格上对扭转初唐浮靡诗风、开启盛唐清新刚健诗风起到先驱作用,在体制上则奠定了五言律诗的基础。本篇便是骆宾王的一首五律佳作。

西陆蝉声唱,南冠客思侵①。
那堪玄鬓影,来对白头吟②。
露重飞难进,风多响易沉③。
无人信高洁,谁为表余心④?

①西陆:指秋天。南冠:楚国的帽子,这里是囚犯的代称。客思:流落他乡而产生的思乡之情。侵:扰。

②玄鬓:指蝉。古代妇女将鬓发梳为蝉翼之状,称为蝉鬓,这里以蝉鬓称蝉。白头吟:乐府曲名。一说"白头"指诗人自己,"吟"指蝉鸣。

③"露重"两句是说,秋露浓重,寒蝉明翅也难以飞进,秋风飒飒,蝉的鸣叫声被风声淹没。

④高洁:古人认为蝉栖息在高树上,餐风饮露,清高纯洁。

Outside a cicada is stridulating in the depths of autumn,
While in jail I am tortured by a surge of homesickness.
Hoary – haired with grief, how can I endure
Such plaintive singing of the black-headed creature?
Heavy dew has encumbered it from taking wing,
Its sounds easily muffled by strong winds.
Nobody in the world trusts my noble and unsullied nature,
Who is there to vindicate my innocence?

唐高宗上元二年(675),王勃往交趾省亲,途经南昌时,正赶上洪州都督举行宴会。王勃参加,并写了本诗及序(即著名的《滕王阁序》)。

滕王阁为唐高祖李渊之子滕王李元婴任洪州(治所在今江西省南昌市)都督时所建。故址在今江西省新建县西章江门上,下临赣江。

滕王高阁临江渚,珮玉鸣鸾罢歌舞①。
画栋朝飞南浦云,珠帘暮卷西山雨②。
闲云潭影日悠悠,物换星移几度秋。
阁中帝子今何在?槛外长江空自流③。

①渚:水边。鸾:刻有鸾鸟形的铃铛。这两句是说,赣江边上高耸的滕王阁,本是滕王欣赏歌舞的场所,滕王去后,歌舞也就停止了。

②南浦:地名,在今江西省南昌市西南。西山:在今江西省南昌市西北,又名南昌山。

③帝子:皇帝的儿子,指滕王。槛:栏杆。长江:指赣江。

The Pavilion of Prince Teng towers high by the riverside,
But gone is the music amid tinkling jade pendants and carriage bells.
Painted pillars loom through the morning cloud from South Bay,
Pearly window curtains flutter in the evening rain from West Hills.
Only lazy clouds and shadows in the water are seen these long days,
Great changes have taken place in the years gone by.
Where is the prince who had the pavilion built here?
Beyond the balustrade silently the long river flows.

本诗是著名的赠别诗。开头两句对起，"三秦"实写，"五津"为虚笔，视野壮阔，引出三、四句言别。最后两联一洗悲酸之态，意气昂扬，尤其"海内存知己，天涯若比邻"一句，境界豪迈、旷达，成为家喻户晓的名句。

"杜少府"是王勃的友人，生平不详；"蜀州"位于今四川省崇庆县。

城阙辅三秦，风烟望五津①。
与君离别意，同是宦游人②。
海内存知己，天涯若比邻③。
无为在岐路，儿女共沾巾④。

①阙(què 确)：皇宫门前两边的楼观(guàn 贯)，也称望楼。城阙：指京城长安。辅：护卫。三秦：今陕西省关中地区，古为秦国，秦亡后，项羽分其地为雍、塞、翟三个王国，故称"三秦"。五津：长江自湔堰至犍为有白华津、万里津、江首津、涉头津、江南津等五渡口，合称"五津"。

②君：指杜少府。宦游人：远离家乡出外作官的人。

③海内：四海之内，指国内。存：恤问，问候。

④无为：不要。岐路：岔路，指离别之处。

110

The capital and palace are guarded by the land of three Qin king-
  doms,①
In the distance the Five Ferries② are screened by wind and mist.
Now comes the time for us to bid farewell to each other,
And we will both be officials away from home on duty.
So long as we remain bosom friends in our heart of hearts,
We'll still feel like neighbours despite the distance apart.
So don't let us shed silly tears like youngsters
At that last moment when we both wave goodbye.

①　In the central part of present-day Shaanxi Province.
②　Alluding to Sichuan Province because of the five big ferries along the
Mingjiang River in the west of the region.

这是杨炯的一首优秀的边塞诗,描写一个书生为平边患而投笔从戎的壮举,洋溢着爱国主义激情和报国之志。"宁为百夫长,胜作一书生"更是初唐四杰和众多盛唐边塞诗人于马背上建功立业的理想的写照。

烽火照西京,心中自不平①。
牙璋辞凤阙,铁骑绕龙城②。
雪暗凋旗画,风多杂鼓声③。
宁为百夫长,胜作一书生④。

①烽火:古代边境发生战争时,用以报警的信号。西京:长安。

②牙璋:古代发兵所用的兵符,有两块,一留朝廷,一给主帅,两相嵌合,作为凭证。嵌合处为牙状,故称牙璋。这里代指将帅奉命出征。凤阙:汉长安建章宫东有凤阙,这里泛指皇宫。铁骑:强悍的骑兵。龙城:汉时匈奴大会祭天之处,故址在今蒙古人民共和国塔米尔河畔。

③凋:凋落,黯淡不明的样子。

④百夫长:卒长,泛指下级军官。

Flaring beacons relayed the alarm to the West Capital,
The scholar was filled with an ardent fighting spirit.
Holding the tally of command the general bade adieu to the palace,
And soon the iron cavalry besieged the Dragon City of Huns.
Army flags faded and dulled in the whirling snow,
While howling winds were punctuated by battle drums.
Better to join the army and be a captain
Than remain a scholar wallowing in books.

王维是盛唐山水田园诗派的代表人物,与孟浩然并称"王孟"。他的思想和创作以 40 岁左右为界限,前期热衷政治,积极进取;后期亦官亦隐,长斋事佛。本诗是其前期之作,写观赏将军射猎,笔力豪放刚健,反映了诗人边塞立功的豪情壮志。

风劲角弓鸣①,将军猎渭城②。
草枯鹰眼疾,雪尽马蹄轻③。
忽过新丰市④,还归细柳营⑤。
回看射雕处⑥,千里暮云平。

①角弓:用牛角装饰的硬弓。

②渭城:秦代的都城咸阳,汉代改称渭城,在今陕西西安市西北渭水北岸。

③"草枯"二句:是说荒原草枯,猎物无所藏身,更显得鹰眼的锐利;残雪被风吹尽,马奔时蹄上没有沾滞,更见出轻捷。

④新丰市:在长安东北,即今陕西省新丰镇。

⑤细柳营:在长安西,为汉代名将周亚夫屯兵处。这里泛指军营。

⑥射雕:据《北史》载,斛律光在洹桥校猎时曾射中一大雕的颈部,被赞为"射雕手"。这里暗用此事美赞将军的武艺。雕,又名鹫,一种飞翔迅捷的猛禽。

A gusty wind, twang of horn-backed bows:
The general is hunting at Weicheng;
Hawks' eyes are keen above the withered grass,
Horse-hooves fall lightly where the snow has melted;
They wheel past Xinfeng Market
And head home to the camp at Xiliu,
Turning once to mark where the vulture fell.
The plain sweeps far off to the evening clouds.

《使至塞上》是王维
著名的送别诗，又称《渭
城曲》或《阳关三叠》。
唐时已谱入乐府，作为
送别之曲，传唱天下。
与盛唐边塞诗人高适的
《别董大》同为送别绝
作，风格却迥然不同，各
领风骚。

单车欲问边，属国过居延①。
征蓬出汉塞，归雁入胡天②。
大漠孤烟直，长河落日圆③。
萧关逢候骑，都护在燕然④。

①单车：一辆车。指独身前
往。问边：察访边关军队。居延：
汉末设县，在今甘肃省张掖县北。
这两句是说，我独自乘车到边塞察
访军情，将要经过汉时的居延属
国。

②征蓬：远飞的蓬草，和下句
的"归雁"一样，皆是作者自喻。

③孤烟直：用狼粪烧的烽烟，
其浓烟聚集直上，微风吹之不斜。

④萧关：在今宁夏回族自治区
固原县东南。候骑（jì季）：侦察骑
兵。都护：都护府的长官，边境最
高的统帅。这里指河西节度使。
燕然：即杭爱山，在今蒙古人民共
和国境内。

A single carriage sets off for the border,
Journeying past the subject state of Juyan;
On we jolt, leaving Han fortresses behind,
A wild goose winging back to the Hunnish sky.
In the great desert one straight plume of smoke,
By the long river at sunset a ball of flame;
Before Xiao Pass we meet a mounted patrol
And learn that our forces have taken Mount Yanran.

这首诗体现了诗、画、乐的结合，无声的静寂、无光的幽暗，一般人都易于觉察，而有声的静寂、有光的幽暗，则较少为人所注意。诗人把握住了空山人语响和深林入返照的一刹那间所显示的特有的幽静境界。

鹿柴(zhài 寨，也写作"砦"，同"寨"，栅栏。)是王维辋川别墅所在地的一个小地名，为养鹿的地方。

空山不见人，
但闻人语响。
返景入深林①，
复照青苔上。

①返景：落日的返照。景，日光。

118

Empty the hills, no man in sight,
Yet voices echo here;
Deep in the woods slanting sunlight
Falls on the jade-green moss.

此诗是唐代最著名的七绝之一。诗为送别友人出使边城安西而作。前人取"柳"、"留"谐音，折长条以赠别。在将分手的客舍前，见此景象，更令人怅触无限。

"元二"是作者的朋友，生平不详；"安西"指唐时所设安西都护府，治所在今新疆库车县。

渭城朝雨浥轻尘①，
客舍青青柳色新。
劝君更尽一杯酒，
西出阳关无故人②。

①浥(yì 邑)：沾湿。
②阳关：汉置，在今甘肃敦煌县西，与玉门关同为通往西域的要道。因在玉门关南面，故称"阳关"。

A morning shower in Weicheng has settled the light dust;
The willows by the hostel are fresh and green;
Come, drink one more cup of wine,
West of the pass you will meet no more old friends.

本诗以雄奇奔放的笔调，博采各种传说和民谣，驰骋丰富的想象，描绘了一幅奇丽惊险的蜀道画卷。流露出作者对人生的感慨和对社会问题的关切，是一首浪漫主义的名作。据说，李白初到京师，贺知章前来探访。李白请他读本诗，尚未读完，贺知章便连连赞叹"谪仙"。

①噫（yī 一）吁（xū 虚）哦（xī 希）：惊叹声。

②危乎高哉：高啊高啊。

③蚕丛、鱼凫（fú 浮）：传说中古蜀国的两个先王。

④茫然：是说蜀国开国久远，其事迹渺茫难详。

⑤"尔来"二句：是说蜀、秦两地长期隔绝。尔来，指从开国以来。四万八千岁，形容时间久远，未必实数。秦塞（sài 赛），犹言秦地。秦中自古称四塞之国。

⑥太白：山名，在今陕西省眉县东南。鸟道：鸟飞的径道。

⑦峨眉：山名，在今四川省峨眉县西南。

⑧"地崩"句：据《华阳国志·蜀志》所载，秦惠王知蜀王好色，特送

噫吁哦①，危乎高哉②！蜀道之难，难于上青天。蚕丛及鱼凫③，开国何茫然④。尔来四万八千岁，不与秦塞通人烟⑤。西当太白有鸟道⑥，可以横绝峨眉巅⑦。地崩山摧壮士死⑧，然后天梯石栈相钩连⑨。上有六龙回日之高标⑩，下有冲波逆折之回川⑪。黄鹤之飞尚不得过，猿猱欲度愁攀援。青泥何盘盘，百步九折萦岩峦。扪参历井仰胁息，以手抚膺坐长叹。问君西游何时还，畏途巉岩不可攀。但见悲鸟号古木，雄飞雌从绕林间。又闻子规啼夜月，愁空山。蜀道之难，难于上青天，使人听此凋朱颜。连峰去天不盈尺，枯松倒挂倚绝壁。飞湍瀑流争喧豗，砯崖转石万壑雷。其险也如此，嗟尔远道之人胡为乎来哉！剑阁峥嵘而崔嵬，一夫当关，万夫莫开。所守或匪亲，化为狼与豺。朝避猛虎，夕避长蛇，磨牙吮血，杀人如麻。锦城虽云乐，不如早还家。蜀道之难，难于上青天，侧身西望长咨嗟！

他五个美女。蜀王派五个大力士去迎接。回到梓潼时，见一大蛇钻入山洞中，五力士共同抓住蛇尾往外拉，忽然间山崩地裂，把五个壮士和美女全埋在底下，山分成了五岭。秦王因此打通了蜀地。

⑨天梯：形容山路陡峭，如登天的梯子。石栈（zhàn 站）：在高山险绝处凿石架木而成的道路。

⑩六龙：古代神话记载，给日神赶车的羲和，每天驾着六条神龙拉的车子，载着太阳在空中运行。回日：是说太阳车至此要迂回绕道而过。高标：指蜀中的最高峰。

⑪逆折：往回倒流。

What heights!
It is easier to climb to Heaven
Than take the Sichuan Road.
Long ago Can Cong and Yu Fu founded the kingdom of Shu;
Forty-eight thousand years went by,
Yet no road linked it with the land of Qin. [1]
Westward from Taibai Mountain [2] only birds
Wander to the summit of Mount Emei [3]
But not until brave men had perished in the great landslide [4]
Were bridges hooked together in the air
And a path hacked through the rocks.
Above, high peaks turn back the sun's chariot drawn by six
 dragons;
Below, the charging waves are caught in whirlpools;

---

[1] Shu, the old name for Western Sichuan, was conquered by the kingdom of Qin in 316 BC.

[2] A mountain west of the capital, Chang'an.

[3] A mountain in Western Sichuan.

[4] There is a legend that King Hui of Qin promised his five daughters to the prince of Shu. Five brave men were sent to fetch them. On the way back they met a huge serpent which fled into a cave. When they tried to pull it out, the mountain crumbled and the men and princesses perished. Since then a rocky path linked the two kingdoms.

①猱(náo 挠)：猿类动物,体矮小,攀缘树木轻捷如飞。

②青泥：岭名,在今陕西略阳县西北,为当时入蜀要道。盘盘：纡回曲折的样子。

③岩峦：山峰。

④扪(mén 门)：抚摸。参(shēn身)、井：均为星宿名。"扪参历井"是说由秦入蜀好似摸到参星,擦过井宿。

⑤君：此指入蜀的友人。西游：指入蜀。

⑥畏途：艰险可怕的道路。巉(chán 蝉)岩：险峻的山石。

⑦号：悲鸣。

⑧子规：即杜鹃鸟,又名杜宇。

⑨凋朱颜：容颜失色。

⑩倚：依。

⑪飞湍(tuān)：如飞的急流。喧豗(huī 灰)：喧闹声。

⑫"砯(pēng 烹)崖"句：是说急流在一道道山沟中奔腾的冲击,使石翻滚,发出雷鸣般的声响。砯,水击岩石声,此作动词冲击解。

噫吁嚱,危乎高哉！蜀道之难,难于上青天。蚕丛及鱼凫,开国何茫然。尔来四万八千岁,不与秦塞通人烟。西当太白有鸟道,可以横绝峨眉巅。地崩山摧壮士死,然后天梯石栈相钩连。上有六龙回日之高标,下有冲波逆折之回川。黄鹤之飞尚不得过,猿猱欲度愁攀援①。青泥何盘盘②,百步九折萦岩峦③。扪参历井仰胁息④,以手抚膺坐长叹。问君西游何时还⑤,畏途巉岩不可攀⑥。但见悲鸟号古木⑦,雄飞雌从绕林间。又闻子规啼夜月,愁空山⑧。蜀道之难,难于上青天,使人听此凋朱颜⑨。连峰去天不盈尺,枯松倒挂倚绝壁⑩。飞湍瀑流争喧豗⑪,砯崖转石万壑雷⑫。其险也如此,嗟尔远道之人胡为乎来哉！剑阁峥嵘而崔嵬,一夫当关,万夫莫开。所守或匪亲,化为狼与豺。朝避猛虎,夕避长蛇,磨牙吮血,杀人如麻。锦城虽云乐,不如早还家。蜀道之难,难于上青天,侧身西望长咨嗟！

Not even yellow cranes dare fly this way,
Monkeys cannot leap those gorges.
At Green Mud Ridge the path winds back and forth,
With nine twists for every hundred steps.
Touching the stars, the traveller looks up and gasps,
Then sinks down, clutching his heart, to groan aloud.
Friend, when will you return from this westward journey?
This is a fearful way. You cannot cross these cliffs.
The only living things are birds crying in ancient trees,
Male wooing female up and down the woods,
And the cuckoo, weary of empty hills,
Singing to the moon.
It is easier to climb to heaven
Than take the Sichuan Road.
The mere telling of its perils blanches youthful cheeks.
Peak follows peak, each but a hand's breadth from the sky;
Dead pine trees hang head down into the chasms,
Torrents and waterfalls outroar each other,
Pounding the cliffs and boiling over rocks,
Booming like thunder through a thousand caverns.

噫吁哦,危乎高哉!蜀道之难,难于上青天。蚕丛及鱼凫,开国何茫然。尔来四万八千岁,不与秦塞通人烟。西当太白有鸟道,可以横绝峨眉巅。地崩山摧壮士死,然后天梯石栈相钩连。上有六龙回日之高标,下有冲波逆折之回川。黄鹤之飞尚不得过,猿猱欲度愁攀援。青泥何盘盘,百步九折萦岩峦。扪参历井仰胁息,以手抚膺坐长叹。问君西游何时还,畏途巉岩不可攀。但见悲鸟号古木,雄飞雌从绕林间。又闻子规啼夜月,愁空山。蜀道之难,难于上青天,使人听此凋朱颜。连峰去天不盈尺,枯松倒挂倚绝壁。飞湍瀑流争喧豗,砯崖转石万壑雷。其险也如此,嗟尔远道之人胡为乎来哉①!剑阁峥嵘而崔嵬②,一夫当关,万夫莫开。所守或匪亲,化为狼与豺③。朝避猛虎,夕避长蛇,磨牙吮血,杀人如麻。锦城虽云乐④,不如早还家。蜀道之难,难于上青天,侧身西望长咨嗟⑤!

①胡为乎:为什么。

②剑阁:大、小剑山之间的一条三十里长的栈道,在今四川剑阁县北。峥嵘:高峻的样子。崔嵬(wéi 围):高险崎岖。

③"一夫"四句:西晋张载《剑阁铭》:"一人荷戟,万夫趦趄(zī 资)趄(jū 居;犹豫不进)。形胜之地,匪亲弗居。"此化用其语,以状剑阁的险要。或匪亲,如果不是可信赖的人。匪,同"非"。一说狼、豺及下两句的猛虎、长蛇,均比喻分裂者或叛乱者。

④锦城:锦官城的简称,即成都,蜀国的都城。

⑤咨(zī 资)嗟(jiē 皆):叹息。

What takes you, traveller, this long, weary way
So filled with danger?
Sword Pass① is steep and narrow,
One man could hold this pass against ten thousand;
And sometimes its defenders
Are not mortal men but wolves and jackals.
By day we dread the savage tiger, by night the serpent,
Sharp-fanged sucker of blood
Who chops men down like stalks of hemp.
The City of Brocade② may be a pleasant place,
But it is best to seek your home.
For it is easier to climb to heaven
Than take the Sichuan Road.
I gaze into the west, and sigh.·

---

① In Northern Sichuan, on the route to Shaanxi where the kingdom of Qin was.

② A name for Chengdu, the capital of Shu.

本诗为李白所作三首《行路难》中的第一首,写于天宝三年(744)李白离开长安的时候。诗中抒发了他在政治道路上遭遇艰难时的愤激情绪;但也未因此放弃其远大的政治理想,表现了他对人生前途乐观豪迈的气概,充满了积极浪漫主义的情调。

金樽清酒斗十千,玉盘珍羞直万钱①。
停杯投箸不能食,拔剑四顾心茫然②。
欲渡黄河冰塞川,将登太行雪满山③。
闲来垂钓碧溪上,忽复乘舟梦日边④。
行路难!行路难!多歧路,今安在⑤?
长风破浪会有时,直挂云帆济沧海⑥。

①樽(zūn 尊):古代装酒的器具。斗十千:一斗酒价值十千钱,极言酒价之高,说明酒很名贵。斗:有柄的盛酒器。羞:同"馐",美味食品。直:同"值",价值。

②箸(zhù 铸):筷子。

③太行:山名,位于今之河南、河北、山西三省之间。

④垂钓碧溪:《史记·齐太公世家》记载,吕尚九十岁时垂钓于磻溪,得遇周文王。梦日边:传说伊尹在将受到成汤的征聘时,梦见乘船经过日月旁边。这两句用吕尚、伊尹的故事,暗示人生遭遇变化无常,暂时闲过一段时间,终有得到重用的一天。

⑤安在:在哪里。

⑥长风破浪:《宋书·宗悫(què 确)传》说,宗悫的叔父问他志向是什么,宗悫说:"愿乘长风破万里浪。"后人用"乘风破浪"比喻施展政治抱负。云帆:像白云般的船帆。济:渡。

Clear wine in golden goblets, ten thousand cash a cup,
And costly delicacies on jade platters.
Yet I spurn drinking and toss away my chopsticks,
Sword in hand, restless, I wonder what to do.
I want to cross the Yellow River, but it's ice-bound;
I want to climb the Taihang Mountains, but they're snow-covered.
So idly I fish by a limpid stream, ①
Dreaming of sailing towards the sun. ②
Travelling is hard! Travelling is hard!
So many crossroads; which to choose?
One day I'll skim the waves, blown by the wind,
With sails hoisted high, across the vast ocean.

---

① Lü Shang used to fish by the Wei River before he met King Wen of Zhou and helped him to conquer the Shangs.

② Yi Yin, before he was discovered by King Tang of Shang, dreamed that he was sailing in a barge towards the sun.

李白思想集儒、仙、侠三者合一。本诗便是这种复杂思想的充分体现,诗人将浪漫主义手法和批判现实主义精神结合起来,豪放、飘逸地描绘出一幅奇谲多变、含蕴丰富的图景。

"天姥(mǔ母)",即天姥山,在今浙江省新昌县东。

海客谈瀛洲,烟涛微茫信难求①。越人语天姥,云霞明灭或可睹②。天姥连天向天横,势拔五岳掩赤城③。天台四万八千丈,对此欲倒东南倾④。我欲因之梦吴越,一夜飞度镜湖月⑤。湖月照我影,送我到剡溪⑥。谢公宿处今尚在,渌水荡漾清猿啼⑦。脚着谢公屐,身登青云梯。半壁见海日,空中闻天鸡。千岩万转路不定,迷花倚石忽已暝。熊咆龙吟殷岩泉,慄深林兮惊层巅。云青青兮欲雨,水澹澹兮生烟。列缺霹雳,丘峦崩摧。洞天石扉,訇然中开。青冥浩荡不见底,日月照耀金银台。霓为衣兮风为马,云之君兮纷纷而来下。虎鼓瑟兮鸾回车,仙之人兮列如麻。忽魂悸以魄动,恍惊起而长嗟。惟觉时之枕席,失向来之烟霞。世间行乐亦如此,古来万事东流水。别君去兮何时还?且放白鹿青崖间,须行即骑访名山。安能摧眉折腰事权贵,使我不得开心颜!

①海客:航海的人。瀛洲:古代传说东海中有蓬莱、方丈、瀛洲三座仙山。微茫:模糊不清的样子。信:确实。

②越:今浙江省一带地方。语:谈论。云霞明灭:指天姥山在云霞中时隐时现。

③拔:超拔。五岳:我国五座大名山的总称,即东岳泰山、西岳华山、南岳衡山、北岳恒山、中岳嵩山。掩:盖过。赤城:山名,在今浙江省天台县北。

④天台:山名,在今浙江省天台县北。此:指天姥山。这两句是说,那四万八千丈高的天台山对着天姥山,像是要拜倒一样地向着东南方向倾倒。

⑤之:这,指代越人对天姥山的谈论。吴越:今江苏省南部及浙江一带地方。镜湖:又名鉴湖或庆湖,在今浙江省绍兴县南。

⑥剡(shàn善)溪:在今浙江省嵊(shèng圣)县南,即曹娥江的上游。

⑦谢公宿处:指南北朝宋代诗人谢灵运当年游览剡溪时的投宿处。清猿啼:清亮的猿啼声。

Seafarers tell of fairy isles;
Lost among mist and waves.
But the men of Yue① speak of Sky-Mother Mountain
Showing herself through rifts in shimmering clouds.
Sky-Mother soars to heaven, spans the horizon,
Towers over the Five Peaks②and the Scarlet Fortress;
While Sky-Terrace, four hundred and eighty thousand feet high,
Staggers southeastward before it.
So, longing in my dreams for Wu and Yue,
One night I flew over Mirror Lake under the moon;
The moon cast my shadow on the water
And travelled with me all the way to Shanxi.
The lodge of Lord Xie③ still remained
Where green waters swirled and the cry of apes was shrill;

① The land of Yue lay in what is now Zhejiang Province, the home of the fa-
mous mountains: Sky-Mother, Scarlet Fortress and Sky-Terrace.

② Five high mountains in China: Mount Tai, Mount Hua, Mount Heng in the
south, Mount Heng in the north and Mount Song.

③ Xie Lingyun, a Jin-dynasty poet who was fond of mountaineering and made
himself special hobnailed shoes for climbing.

①谢公屐(jī积):是谢灵运特制的一种专供游山用的木鞋,底下装有活动的齿,上山时抽去前齿,下山时抽去后齿。青云梯:高峻陡峭的山路,好象是登攀青天的梯子。

②半壁:半山腰。海日:海中升起的太阳。闻天鸡:指天亮了。《述异记》说我国东南边有桃都山,山上长着一种名桃都的大树,树上有天鸡,每天早晨,阳光一照到桃都树上,天鸡就叫起来,于是天下的鸡都跟着叫起来。

③暝(míng明):日落天黑。

④殷(yǐn引):震动。层巅:层层的山峰。

⑤云青青:形容云层的浓厚。水澹澹(dàn淡):形容水波荡漾。

⑥列缺:闪电。霹雳:雷。

⑦洞天:神仙的居处。石扉(fēi非):石门。訇(hōng烘)然:巨大的响声。

⑧青冥:青色的天空。金银台:用金银装饰的仙宫楼台。

⑨云之君:云神。

海客谈瀛洲,烟涛微茫信难求。越人语天姥,云霞明灭或可睹。天姥连天向天横,势拔五岳掩赤城。天台四万八千丈,对此欲倒东南倾。我欲因之梦吴越,一夜飞度镜湖月。湖月照我影,送我到剡溪。谢公宿处今尚在,渌水荡漾清猿啼。脚着谢公屐①,身登青云梯①。半壁见海日,空中闻天鸡②。千岩万转路不定,迷花倚石忽已暝③。熊咆龙吟殷岩泉,慄深林兮惊层巅④。云青青兮欲雨,水澹澹兮生烟⑤。列缺霹雳,丘峦崩摧⑥。洞天石扉,訇然中开⑦。青冥浩荡不见底,日月照耀金银台⑧。霓为衣兮风为马,云之君兮纷纷而来下⑨。虎鼓瑟兮鸾回车,仙之人兮列如麻。忽魂悸以魄动,恍惊起而长嗟。惟觉时之枕席,失向来之烟霞。世间行乐亦如此,古来万事东流水。别君去兮何时还?且放白鹿青崖间,须行即骑访名山。安能摧眉折腰事权贵,使我不得开心颜!

Donning the shoes of Xie,
I climbed the dark ladder of clouds.
Midway, I saw the sun rise from the sea,
Heard the Cock of Heaven crow. ①
And my path twisted through a thousand crags,
Enchanted by flowers I leaned against a rock,
And suddenly all was dark.
Growls of bears and snarls of dragons echoed
Among the rocks and streams;
The deep forest appalled me, I shrank from the lowering cliffs;
Dark were the clouds, heavy with rain;
Waters boiled into misty spray;
Lightning flashed; thunder roared;
Peaks tottered, boulders crashed;
And the stone gate of a great cavern
Yawned open.
Below me, a bottomless void of blue,
Sun and moon gleaming on terraces of silver and gold;
With rainbows for garments, and winds for horses,
The lords of the clouds descended, a mighty host.
Phoenixes circled the chariots, tigers played zithers,
As the immortals went by, rank upon rank.

---

① According to Chinese mythology, this cock roosted on a great tree in the southeast. When the sun rose it crowed, and all the cocks in the world followed suit.

海客谈瀛洲,烟涛微茫信难求。越人语天姥,云霞明灭或可睹。天姥连天向天横,势拔五岳掩赤城。天台四万八千丈,对此欲倒东南倾。我欲因之梦吴越,一夜飞度镜湖月。湖月照我影,送我到剡溪。谢公宿处今尚在,渌水荡漾清猿啼。脚着谢公屐,身登青云梯。半壁见海日,空中闻天鸡。千岩万转路不定,迷花倚石忽已暝。熊咆龙吟殷岩泉,慄深林兮惊层巅。云青青兮欲雨,水澹澹兮生烟。列缺霹雳,丘峦崩摧。洞天石扉,訇然中开。青冥浩荡不见底,日月照耀金银台。霓为衣兮风为马,云之君兮纷纷而来下。虎鼓瑟兮鸾回车,仙之人兮列如麻①。忽魂悸以魄动,恍惊起而长嗟②。惟觉时之枕席,失向来之烟霞③。世间行乐亦如此,古来万事东流水④。别君去兮何时还?且放白鹿青崖间,须行即骑访名山⑤。安能摧眉折腰事权贵⑥,使我不得开心颜!

①回车:回转车子。即驾着车子。

②悸:惊怕。恍(huǎng 谎):同"恍",心神不定的样子。长嗟:长声叹息。

③觉:醒。向来:刚才。烟霞:指梦游中的幻境。

④亦如此:也如同梦中的景象变化莫测。

⑤君:指在山东漫游时结交的朋友。白鹿:传说中神仙的一种代步的神兽。

⑥摧眉折腰:低眉弯腰。事:侍奉,伺候。

My heart was seized by fear and wonder,
And waking with a start I cried out,
For nothing was there except my mat and pillow —
Gone was the world of mists and clouds.
And so with the plesures of this life;
All pass, as water flows eastward.
I leave you, friend — when shall I return?
I shall pasture white stags among green peaks
And ride to visit mountains famed in legend.
Would you have me bow my head before mighty princes,
Forgetting all the joy of my heart?

孟浩然与李白是同时期的著名诗人。李白在安陆居住时结识了他，很仰慕其气节，在《赠孟浩然》一诗中写下了"吾爱孟夫子，风流天下闻"的诗句。本诗则通过送别孟浩然时对景物的描述，抒发依依惜别之情。

"黄鹤楼"旧址在今湖北省武汉市武昌桥头黄鹤矶上；"广陵"位于今江苏省扬州市。

故人西辞黄鹤楼，
烟花三月下扬州①。
孤帆远影碧空尽②，
唯见长江天际流。

①西辞：黄鹤楼在广陵之西，孟浩然由西去东，所以说"西辞"。烟花：指桃花盛开的绚烂景色。

②碧空尽：在碧色的天空中消逝了。

At Yellow Crane Tower in the west
My old friend says farewell;
In the mist and flowers of spring
He goes down to Yangzhou; ①
Lonely sail, distant shadow,
Vanish in blue emptiness;
All I see is the great river
Flowing into the far horizon.

①　Also known as Guangling at that time.

　　高适是盛唐著名的边塞诗人,与岑参并称"高岑"。此诗是对王之涣《凉州词》"黄河远上白云间"的唱和,也由音乐起兴,抒写征夫远戍思乡之情,委婉蕴藉,意境高远,韵味无穷。

霜净胡天牧马还,
月明羌笛戍楼间①。
借问梅花何处落②,
风吹一夜满关山。

①"霜净"两句说,霜后的边塞,秋高气爽,在牧马已还的明月之夜,士兵们吹起悦耳的羌笛。
②梅花:《梅花落》曲的简称。

Snow has thawed in the borderlands, grazing horses returned,
A flute melody hovers amid moonlit watchtowers.
Where is the tune of *Fallen Plum Blossom* played?
It wafts through the borderlands on the night wind.

李白《战城南》有云:"乃知兵者是凶器,圣人不得已而用之",以战场惨况来揭露战争的残酷。本篇以重墨全方位地反映了战争带给人民的深重苦难。诗中未有直斥战争之罪,而笔调沉郁,深情叹惋,弥见深刻有力。乃知"诗史"之誉,其来有自。

车辚辚①,马萧萧②,行人弓箭各在腰③。耶娘妻子走相送④,尘埃不见咸阳桥⑤。牵衣顿足拦道哭,哭声直上干云霄⑥。道旁过者问行人,行人但云点行频⑦。或从十五北防河,便至四十西营田⑧。去时里正与裹头⑨,归来头白还戍边。边庭流血成海水,武皇开边意未已⑩。君不闻汉家山东二百州⑪,千村万落生荆杞⑫。纵有健妇把锄犁,禾生陇亩无东西。况复秦兵耐苦战,被驱不异犬与鸡。长者虽有问,役夫敢申恨?且如今年冬,未休关西卒。县官急索租,租税从何出?信知生男恶,反是生女好;生女犹得嫁比邻,生男埋没随百草!君不见青海头,古来白骨无人收。新鬼烦冤旧鬼哭,天阴雨湿声啾啾!

①辚(lín 林)辚:车辆走动声。

②萧萧:马鸣声。

③行人:指被征出发的战士。

④耶:同爷,父亲。妻子:妻子及子女。

⑤"尘埃"句:是说沿路灰尘弥漫,咸阳桥也看不见了。咸阳桥,即中渭桥,故址在原陕西咸阳县西南渭水上。

⑥干:冲上。

⑦但云:只说。点行频:征调频繁。点行,按户籍点招壮丁。

⑧"或从"二句是说,有的人十五岁起就远戍西北,直到四十岁还没回家。北防河、西营田,均泛指西北边防。营田,屯田。

⑨里正:里长。唐制百户为一里,设里正。与裹头:替壮丁扎头巾。说明当时壮丁年幼。

⑩武皇:汉武帝。此借指唐玄宗。开边:用武力扩张疆土。

⑪汉家:借指唐朝。山东:指华山以东。二百州:唐代潼关以东有七道,共二百十七州,此约举整数。诗中实指关东以外广大地区。

⑫荆杞(qǐ 启):荆棘和杞柳。此泛指野生灌木。

Carts rumbling, horses neighing,

Men march with bows and arrows at their waists;

Parents, wives and children are there to see them off,

And Xianyang Bridge is swallowed up in dust;

Stamping and clutching the men's clothes, blocking the road, they
    weep;

The sound of weeping rises to the clouds.

In answer to a passerby

The marchers say, "We're conscripts once again!

At fifteen some of us went north to guard the Yellow River;

Now forty, we are being sent to open waste land in the west.

When we left, the headman bound our head-cloths on;

White-haired and just home, we are off to the frontier again!

Seas of blood have been shed at the frontier,

Yet still the emperor seeks to swell his realm.

It's said, in two hundred districts east of the Pass

Thousands of villages grow thick with brambles;

车辚辚,马萧萧,行人弓箭各在腰。耶娘妻子走相送,尘埃不见咸阳桥。牵衣顿足拦道哭,哭声直上干云霄。道旁过者问行人,行人但云点行频。或从十五北防河,便至四十西营田。去时里正与裹头,归来头白还戍边。边庭流血成海水,武皇开边意未已。君不闻汉家山东二百州,千村万落生荆杞。纵有健妇把锄犁,禾生陇亩无东西①。况复秦兵耐苦战②,被驱不异犬与鸡。长者虽有问,役夫敢申恨?且如今年冬,未休关西卒③。县官急索租,租税从何出?信知生男恶,反是生女好;生女犹得嫁比邻,生男埋没随百草!君不见青海头④,古来白骨无人收。新鬼烦冤旧鬼哭,天阴雨湿声啾啾⑤!

①"禾生"句:是说田里的庄稼种得不成行列。

②秦兵:关中兵。关中为古秦地。此指眼前被征调的壮丁。

③未休:指征调不止。关西卒:即"秦兵"。函谷关以西称关西。

④青海头:青海湖边,在今青海东部,唐军与吐蕃常在此作战。

⑤啾(jiū 纠)啾:古人想象中的鬼哭声。

Even where sturdy women plough and hoe,
The crops are straggling in the ragged fields;
Since we of the northwest are seasoned fighters,
We are driven like dogs or hens.
You, sir, may show concern,
But how dare we soldiers complain?
Yet only this very winter
Troops west of the Pass had no rest;
The magistrate is plaguing us for taxes,
But where are taxes to come from?
We know now it is bad to bear sons,
Better to have daughters;
For a girl can be married to a next-door neighbour,
But a boy will perish like the grass in the field.
Have you not seen, beside Lake Kokonor,
Bleached bones, unburied from ancient times?
There new ghosts curse their fate and old ghosts wail;
In darkness and in rain you hear their sobbing."

《石壕吏》、《潼关吏》与《新安吏》并称"三吏"，是杜甫"诗史"中现实主义作品的高峰。而本诗又是"三吏"中最深刻、最动人的一篇，通过对老妪一家苦难遭遇的描写，反映了安史之乱中人民的深重苦难，体现了诗人"穷年忧黎民"的精神。

暮投石壕村①，有吏夜捉人。老翁逾墙走，老妇出门看②。吏呼一何怒，妇啼一何苦！听妇前致词："三男邺城戍③，一男附书至④，二男新战死。存者且偷生，死者长已矣⑤！室中更无人，惟有乳下孙⑥。有孙母未去，出入无完裙⑦。老妪力虽衰，请从吏夜归。急应河阳役，犹得备晨炊。"夜久语声绝，如闻泣幽咽。天明登前途，独与老翁别。

①投：投宿。石壕村：在今河南省陕县东。

②逾(yú余)：越。走：跑。

③邺城：即相州，今河南省安阳县。戍：守卫。

④附书：托人捎家信。

⑤长已矣：人死不能复生，永远完了。

⑥乳下孙：还在吃奶的孙儿。

⑦母：指小孩的母亲。

One sunset I came to the village of Shihao,
And shortly after there followed
An official, seizing conscripts.
In the courtyard of the peasant's house where I stayed,
An old man climbed quickly over the wall, and vanished.

To the door came his old wife to greet the official.
How fiercely he swore at her,
And how bitterly she cried!
"I have had three sons taken
To be soldiers at Yecheng.
Then came a letter, saying
Two had been killed, and that the third
Never knew which day he might die.
Now in this hut is left
None but a baby grandson
Whose mother still suckles him. . .
She cannot go out, as she has no clothes
To cover her nakedness.

暮投石壕村,有吏夜捉人。老翁逾墙走,老妇出门看。吏呼一何怒,妇啼一何苦!听妇前致词:"三男邺城戍,一男附书至,二男新战死。存者且偷生,死者长已矣!室中更无人,惟有乳下孙。有孙母未去,出入无完裙。老妪力虽衰,请从吏夜归①。急应河阳役,犹得备晨炊②。"夜久语声绝,如闻泣幽咽③。天明登前途,独与老翁别④。

①妪(yù 玉):年老的妇人。此为"听妇"自称。

②河阳:孟津,在黄河北岸,今河南省孟县。

③夜久:夜深。泣幽咽:极为悲伤而吞声哭泣。

④登前途:登程上路。

All I can do is to go back with you
To the battle at Heyang.
There I can cook for you,
Even though I am weak and old..."

Night wore on.
The sound of voices died away
Until there was left, coming from the hut,
Only the sobbing of the daughter-in-law.
At dawn I rose and left,
With only the old man
To bid me goodbye.

这是一首赞美自然景物的小诗。构思精巧,既为写春雨,便"无一字不是春雨,无一笔不是春夜喜雨"(查慎行语);且炼字极新奇精当,"潜"、"细"、"湿"、"重"一向为人称道,充分体现了杜诗"语不惊人死不休"的语言特点和深厚功力。

好雨知时节,当春乃发生①。
随风潜入夜,润物细无声。
野径云俱黑,江船火独明②。
晓看红湿处,花重锦官城③。

①当春:正当春天需要雨的时候。

②野径:田野间的道路。

③花重:花朵因饱含雨水而沉重。红湿:指花带雨水而湿。锦官城:今四川省成都市的别称。

A good rain knows its season
And comes when spring is here;
On the heels of the wind it slips secretly into the night,
Silent and soft, it moistens everything.
Now clouds hang black above the country roads,
A lone boat on the river sheds a glimmer of light;
At dawn we shall see splashes of rain-washed red —
Drenched, heavy blooms in the City of Brocade. ①

---

① Another name for Chengdu.

作者真实地记录了所居成都草堂屋顶被狂风吹破后的狼狈情景,又从自己眼前的困苦生活联想到丧乱以来的颠沛流离,并推己及人,转而同情天下寒士的痛苦,由衷地希望出现万千广厦庇护天下寒士,自己受冻而死也心甘情愿,是诗人忧国忧民思想的真实写照。

八月秋高风怒号,卷我屋上三重茅①。茅飞渡江洒江郊,高者挂罥长林梢②,下者飘转沉塘坳③。南村群童欺我老无力,忍能对面为盗贼④。公然抱茅入竹去⑤,唇焦口燥呼不得⑥,归来倚杖自叹息。俄顷风定云墨色⑦,秋天漠漠向昏黑⑧。布衾多年冷似铁,娇儿恶卧踏里裂⑨。床头屋漏无干处,雨脚如麻未断绝。自经丧乱少睡眠⑩,长夜沾湿何由彻⑪!安得广厦千万间,大庇天下寒士俱欢颜⑫,风雨不动安如山!呜呼!何时眼前突兀见此屋⑬,吾庐独破受冻死亦足!

①三重茅:几层茅草,是虚指。

②罥(juàn 绢):挂。长:高。

③塘坳:低洼积水处。

④忍能:怎忍心?

⑤竹:指竹林。

⑥呼不得:喝不住。

⑦俄顷:一会儿。

⑧漠漠:阴沉沉、灰蒙蒙的样子。

⑨恶卧:睡相不好。里:被里子。

⑩丧乱:此指安史之乱。

⑪何由彻:怎么才能挨到天亮。彻:彻晓。

⑫庇(bì 毕):遮盖护住。

⑬突兀:高耸的样子。见:同"现"。

The eighth month and a mid-autumn gale
Tore off the three layers of my thatch;
Across the stream flew the straw to scatter the banks,
Caught high up on tall trees
Or fluttering down into the pools and ditches.
The village boys found a feeble old man easy game,
And robbed me to my face,
Openly lugging off armfuls through the bamboos,
Though I shouted till I was hoarse and my lips parched.
I went home then, leaning on my stick, and sighed.

Soon the wind fell and black clouds gathered,
The autumn sky grew dark as dusk came on;
My quilt after years of use is cold as iron,
With rents kicked in it by my spoiled, restless son;
The roof, no patch of it dry, leaks over my bed
And the rain streams through like unending strands of hemp;
Ever since the rebellion I have been losing sleep;
Wet through, how can I last out this long night till dawn?

Oh, for a great mansion with ten thousand rooms
Where all the poor on earth could find welcome shelter,
Steady through every storm, secure as a mountain!
Ah, were such a building to spring up before me,
I would freeze to death in my wrecked hut well content.

岑参是唐代创作边塞诗最多、最杰出的诗人。个性"好奇",其边塞诗想象丰富,气势奔放,以慷慨报国的英雄气概和不畏艰苦的乐观主义精神为基本特征。诗风雄奇瑰丽,富于浪漫主义色彩。本诗是其代表作。

"武判官"为作者友人,生平不详。

北风卷地白草折,胡天八月即飞雪①。
忽如一夜春风来,千树万树梨花开。
散入珠帘湿罗幕,狐裘不暖锦衾薄②。
将军角弓不得控,都护铁衣冷难着③。
瀚海阑干百丈冰,愁云惨淡万里凝④。
中军置酒饮归客,胡琴琵琶与羌笛⑤。
纷纷暮雪下辕门,风掣红旗冻不翻⑥。
轮台东门送君去,去时雪满天山路⑦。
山回路转不见君,雪上空留马行处。

①白草:芨芨草,产于西北地区,秋天变白。

②锦衾(qīn 钦):锦缎被子。

③角弓:用牛角装饰的硬弓。控:拉。

④瀚海:大戈壁。阑干:纵横的样子。惨淡:昏暗无光。

⑤中军:本义指主帅亲率的军队,这里指主帅所居的营帐。"胡琴"句,指席间演奏各种器乐佐酒。

⑥辕门:古代多用战车作战,扎营时常以战车首尾相接,围成栅栏,出入处车辕竖立相向作门,称为辕门。翻:翻卷飘扬。

⑦轮台:唐贞观十四年所设三县,取汉轮台为名,隶属北庭都护府。即今新疆乌鲁木齐市米泉县。天山:一名祁连山,位于新疆中部。

The north wind scrapes the ground, the fleabane destroyed,
In the borderlands it starts snowing in the eighth month.
As though a gust of spring wind swept past overnight,
Bringing thousands upon thousands of pear trees into bloom.
It penetrates pearl blinds and moistens silk curtains,
The fox fur is cold, the brocade quilt too thin for the nip.
The general fails to draw steadily his horn-backed bow,
The viceroy can hardly put on his frigid armour.
A vast expanse of desert is covered with ice of a thousand feet,
Gloomy clouds hang over ten thousand miles of frozen land.
In the central camp a homebound colleague is wined and dined,
Music is played with fiddles, lutes and piccolos.
Evening snow keeps coming down at the camp gate,
Wind tugs at the red standard but it's too frozen to flutter.
At the eastern city gate of Luntai[①]I shall see you off,
The road ahead along Tianshan Mountains[②] is heavy with snow.
As the path winds around the mountain and you are out of sight,
Tracks of your horse's hoofs will be left vainly in the snow.

---

①   In present-day Miquan County, Xinjiang Uygur Autonomous Region.

②   A big mountain chain ranging from east to west across the central part of Xinjiang Uygur Autonomous Region.

全诗用大半篇幅叙述老农家贫、耕种薄田,收成不好,还把仅有的一点粮食交了官税,到岁末只好让儿子到山上收橡子充饥。最后两句用老农夫叙述商人用肉养犬,形成了与山农生活的鲜明对比,唱出了老农的痛苦与不平。

老农家贫在山住,耕种山田三四亩。
苗疏税多不得食,输入官仓化为土①。
岁暮锄犁傍空室,呼儿登山收橡实②。
西江贾客珠百斛,船中养犬长食肉③。

①苗疏:指因土地瘠薄,禾苗长得稀疏。化为土:指粮食在官仓中积压腐烂,成了尘土。

②岁暮:年底。傍:靠。橡实:橡树的果实。

③西江:长江上游的一段。贾(gǔ古)客:商人。

In the hills lives a poor old peasant
Farming a few small patches of hilly land;
Sparse his crops, many the taxes, and he goes hungry
While grain in the state granaries turns to dust;
At the year's end his home is bare but for plough and hoe,
He takes his son up the mountain to gather acorns;
But the West River merchant has hundreds of bushels of pearls
And the dog on his boat gorges everyday on meat.

这是一首新题乐府诗,生动形象地叙述了纤夫挽船的困苦生活。被迫挽船的纤夫们"水宿沙行",像海鸟一般。逆水拖船十分艰难,路途遥远,再加上雨雪天气,痛苦难忍。纤夫们又不愿离开父母之乡,于是幻想大水变平田。然而幻想又怎能改变这可悲的命运呢?

苦哉生长当驿边,官家使我牵驿船①。
辛苦日多乐日少,水宿沙行如海鸟②。
逆风上水万斛重,前驿迢迢波淼淼③。
半夜缘堤雪和雨,受他驱遣还复去④。
寒夜衣湿披短蓑,臆穿足裂忍痛何⑤?
到明辛苦无处说,齐声腾踏牵船歌⑥。
一间茅屋何所值? 父母之乡去不得⑦。
我愿此水作平田,长使水夫不怨天。

①驿:驿站。

②水宿沙行:指纤夫夜宿船上,白日在沙洲上拉纤行走。

③斛(hú 胡):量器名,古以十斗为斛,后又以五斗为斛。淼淼(miǎo 秒):水势广远的样子。

④缘堤:指顺着堤走。他:指官家。

⑤臆穿:指纤绳在胸前磨擦,把胸口快磨破了。忍痛何:除了忍受还有什么办法?

⑥到明:到天亮时。腾踏:腾步踏地。

⑦父母之乡:故乡。

156

Pity me, born by a river port,
Conscripted onto two boats.
Hard days are many, good days few,
Like a seagull I sleep on the waves and trudge on sand.
Towed upstream against the wind the boat weighs a hundred tons,
But the last stage and the next are poles apart;
At midnight we reach the dike in snow and sleet,
Out we're driven again as soon as we return.
Cold at night, wet through below our short coir capes,
Lungs bursting, feet bleeding — the pain is hard to bear.
Dawn breaks, but who will listen to our tale of woe?
Together we strain forward — yo-heave-ho!
A thatched hut may be worthless,
But what man can leave the home of his parents?
If I could change this water into land,
Then boatmen need no longer curse their fate.

这首诗借古说今，描绘了西晋灭吴的战事，点出"萧萧芦荻秋"的萧杀背景，含蓄地道出了唐朝岌岌可危的险境。诗章结构严谨，如行云流水，有一气呵成之感，白居易称之为"骊珠"，并非过誉。

"西塞山"位于今湖北省黄石市东。

王濬楼船下益州，金陵王气黯然收①。
千寻铁锁沉江底，一片降幡出石头②。
人世几回伤往事，山形依旧枕寒流③。
今逢四海为家日，故垒萧萧芦荻秋④。

①王濬（jùn 俊）：西晋武帝时益州刺史。楼船：大型战船。益州：州治在今四川省成都市。金陵：今江苏省南京市。

②寻：古代八尺为一寻。铁锁：吴国知道晋将来攻，在长江险要处装置铁锁链以阻止晋水军，王濬用火炬烧毁了铁锁链，战船直抵石头城。降幡：表示投降的旗帜。

③往事：这里指东吴、东晋，及宋、齐、梁、陈破亡的历史。山形：指西塞山。枕：靠。寒流：指长江。

④四海为家：指国家统一。故垒：过去作战的营垒，这里指西塞山。萧萧：风声。芦荻秋：指秋风萧瑟，一片荒凉冷落景象。荻（dí 笛），芦苇一类植物。

Wang Jun's galleons sailed down from Yizhou,[1]
Jinling's[2] kingly grandeur faded sadly away:
Chain-barricades sank fathoms deep in the Yangtze,
Flags of surrender overspread the City of Stone[3].
Time and again men may lament the past;
The mountain remains unchanged, couched above cold river.
Now all within the Four Seas are one family,
By old ramparts autumn wind soughs through the reeds.

---

[1]   Wang Jun (AD 206-285) led the troops of Jin down the Yangtze River from Sichuan to conquer the Kingdom of Wu in AD 279.

[2]   Jinling, present-day Nanjing in Jiangsu Province, was the capital of the Kingdom of Wu (AD 222 – 280) during the Three Kingdoms Period.

[3]   City of Stone was another name for present-day Nanjing.

唐敬宗宝历二年(826),和白居易在扬州相逢,白给刘禹锡写了一首诗,对他所遭贬斥表示不平,刘用此诗作答。诗中回顾了贬谪生活,感情沉郁,但最后表示要重振起精神。其中"沉舟侧畔千帆过,病树前头万木春"一句是全诗之眼,也是千古流传之警语。

巴山楚水凄凉地,二十三年弃置身①。
怀旧空吟闻笛赋,到乡翻似烂柯人②。
沉舟侧畔千帆过,病树前头万木春③。
今日听君歌一曲,暂凭杯酒长精神④。

①巴山楚水:泛指四川、湖广一带。二十三年:刘禹锡于唐顺宗永贞元年(805)九月被贬,到唐敬宗宝历二年(826)被召回,前后近二十三年。弃置:指被贬谪。

②怀旧:怀念老朋友。闻笛赋:指晋向秀所作《思旧赋》。翻似:倒好像。烂柯人:据《述异记》载,晋代王质入山砍柴,遇见两个童子下棋,便停下来观看,棋还没有终局,见斧柄已烂,回到乡里,已过了百年,同时人都已死去。这里表现人世沧桑之感。

③侧畔:旁边。病树:指枯朽的树。万木春:指万木欣欣向荣,生机勃发。这两句比喻自己在政治上遭受打击,心中固然惆怅,却又相当达观,表现出豁达的情怀。

④君:指白居易。歌一曲:指白居易所作《醉后赠刘二十八使君》。

Cold and lonely the mountains of Ba, the rivers of Chu,[1]
Twenty-three years in exile,
Missing old friends, in vain I sang
The song of him who heard fluting,[2]
And home again I am like the woodcutter[3]
Who found his axe-handle rotted.
By the sunken barge a thousand sails go past,
Before the withered tree all is green in spring;
Hearing your song today, sir,
I drink a cup of wine and take fresh heart.

---

[1]   The mountains of Ba and the rivers of Chu referred to far-off regions in southwest China.

[2]   The singer who heard fluting was Xiang Xiu of the third century, who was reminded by flute music of his dead friends and wrote a poem about them. Here Liu Yuxi was thinking of Wang Shuwen and others of his associates who had died.

[3]   The woodcutter was Wang Zhi. According to a Jin-dynasty story, he went into the mountains to cut wood and stayed for a while with some immortals, returning home later only to find that his axe-handle had rotted away and all his neighbours were dead.

这首《杨柳枝词》是刘禹锡创作的民歌体小诗之一。作品保持了清新开朗的民间情调,以俚歌俗调绘真景、抒真情,语言清新朴素,格调自然优美,具有浓郁的地方色彩及别样的生活情趣。

塞北梅花羌笛吹,
淮南桂树小山词①。
请君莫奏前朝曲,
听唱新翻《杨柳枝》。

①塞北:指我国北方边塞地区。梅花:指汉乐府民歌横吹曲的《梅花落》,到了唐代已经过时陈旧。羌笛:我国古代少数民族羌族的一种乐器。淮南小山:旧说为西汉时淮南王刘安的门客。桂树:指《楚辞·招隐士》,其第一句为"桂树丛生兮山之幽"。这两句是说,塞北用羌笛吹奏的《梅花落》,淮南小山的《招隐士》都已陈旧。

North of the Pass, Qiang flutes played *Plum Blossom* ; ①
South of the Huai, Xiao Shan sang *Fragrant Cassia* ②
Play no more tunes, sir, of bygone dynasties
But listen to the new *Willow Ballads*.

---

① The Qiangs were a nomadic people in China's northwest. *Plum Blossom* was a local folk melody.

② Xiao Shan, a protégé of the Prince of Huainan (179-122 BC), wrote a poem in the traditional local style about fragrant cassia.

卖炭翁·白居易(772—846)

白居易为中唐新乐府运动的领袖,反对吟风弄月的文风,主张"文章合为时而著,歌诗合为事而作",即强调诗歌的批判现实主义精神,主张诗歌反映现实,对社会、百姓、时政等发挥积极作用。本诗便是其新乐府代表作,体现了作者"惟歌生民病"的创作态度。

苦宫市也①。

卖炭翁,伐薪烧炭南山中②,满面尘灰烟火色,两鬓苍苍十指黑。卖炭得钱何所营③?身上衣裳口中食。可怜身上衣正单,心忧炭贱愿天寒。夜来城外一尺雪,晓驾炭车辗冰辙④。牛困人饥日已高,市南门外泥中歇。翩翩两骑来是谁?黄衣使者白衫儿⑤。手把文书口称敕,回车叱牛牵向北⑥。一车炭,千余斤,宫使驱将惜不得⑦。半匹红纱一丈绫,系向牛头充炭直⑧。

①作者自注。宫市:德宗贞元末年,宦官到市场上购买宫中所需的物品,看到其需要的东西,就口称"宫市"拿走,或象征性地给点钱,实际上是公开抢掠民间财物,所以市民看到他们就关门逃避。

②伐薪:砍柴。南山:终南山,位于陕西省长安县南。

③营:谋。

④冰辙:冰雪冻结的车路。

⑤黄衣使者:宦官。唐代品级较高的宦官穿黄衣。白衫儿:指宦官中没有品级的随从。

⑥把:拿。文书:公文。敕(chì赤):皇帝的命令。回车:拉转车子。叱牛:大声吆喝牛。牵向北:往北牵,唐皇宫在长安城的北部,东西两市在南边,所以要把牛往北牵。

⑦宫使:指宦官。驱:赶走。将:语助词。

⑧半匹:即二丈。绫:一种很薄的丝织品。充炭直:作为一车炭的代价。直,同"值",价钱。

164

The old man who sells charcoal
Cuts wood and fires his wares on the South Hill,
His face streaked with dust and ashes, grimed with smoke,
His temples grizzled, his ten fingers blackened.
The little money he makes is hardly enough
For clothing for his back, food for his belly;
But though his coat is thin he hopes for winter —
Cold weather will keep up the price of fuel.
At night a foot of snow falls outside the city,
At dawn his charcoal cart crushes ruts in the ice;
By the time the sun is high,
The ox is tired out and the old man hungry,
They rest in the slush outside the south gate of the market.
Then up canter two riders; who can they be?
Palace heralds in yellow jackets and white shirts;
They wave a decree, shout that these are imperial orders;
Then turn the cart, hoot at the ox and drag it north.
A whole cartload of charcoal, more than a thousand catties,
Yet they drive it off to the palace and he must accept
The strip of red gauze and the ten feet of silk
Which they fasten to the ox's horns as payment!

乐天以写实见称于世,而此诗显然有着浓厚的浪漫主义色彩。固知名家擅技,不特一端。诗中虽对明皇耽色误国有所微词,着眼仍在以典丽的辞句歌颂这种恋情。帝王后妃之情,而能传于千古,确是拜受此诗之赐。

汉皇重色思倾国①,御宇多年求不得②。
杨家有女初长成③,养在深闺人未识④。
天生丽质难自弃⑤,一朝选在君王侧⑥。
回眸一笑百媚生⑦,六宫粉黛无颜色⑧。
春寒赐浴华清池⑨,温泉水滑洗凝脂⑩。
侍儿扶起娇无力⑪,始是新承恩泽时⑫。
云鬓花颜金步摇⑬,芙蓉帐暖度春宵⑭。

①汉皇:汉武帝刘彻,这里用来借指唐玄宗李隆基。倾国:美艳女子的代称,即绝代佳人的意思。

②御宇:统治天下。

③杨家有女:指杨玉环,即杨贵妃。蒲州永乐(今山西永济县)人,开元二十三年(735)册封为玄宗之子寿王李瑁的妃子,后被玄宗看中,于开元二十八年(740)让她先出家度为女道士,住太真宫,赐名太真。至天宝四年(745)才正式将她纳入宫中,册封为贵妃。

④“养在深闺”句:杨玉环早做了寿王的妃子,这里所谓“养在深闺”,是诗人的曲笔,诗人不便把玄宗夺儿子寿王的妃子的事说出来,必然要为尊者讳。

⑤丽质:美丽的容貌。难自弃:不容许她辜负自己的“丽质”。

⑥一朝:一天。

⑦回眸(móu 谋):闪动眼珠。眸:眼中瞳人,泛指眼珠。

⑧六宫:泛指后妃的住处。粉黛:原是妇女的化妆品,粉是擦脸的,黛是画眉的,这里的粉黛是宫中妇女的代称。无颜色:是说宫中妇女和美丽的杨贵妃相比,脸上显得毫无光彩。

⑨华清池:在今陕西省临潼县东南骊山上。

⑩凝脂:指杨贵妃肌肤洁白细嫩,如同凝聚的脂肪。

⑪侍儿:服侍杨贵妃的宫女。

⑫始是:才是。新承恩泽:开始得到玄宗的宠爱。

⑬金步摇:妇女用的首饰,上有垂珠,行步时就摇动。

⑭芙蓉帐:带有荷花图案的帐子。

Appreciating feminine charms,
The Han emperor sought a great beauty.
Throughout his empire he searched
For many years without success.
Then a daughter of the Yang family
Matured to womanhood.
Since she was secluded in her chamber,
None outside had seen her.
Yet with such beauty bestowed by fate,
How could she remain unknown?
One day she was chosen
To attend the emperor.
Glancing back and smiling,
She revealed a hundred charms.
All the powdered ladies of the six palaces
At once seemed dull and colourless.
One cold spring day she was ordered
To bathe in the Huaqing Palace baths.
The warm water slipped down
Her glistening jade-like body.
When her maids helped her rise,
She looked so frail and lovely,
At once she won the emperor's favour.
Her hair like a cloud,
Her face like a flower,
A gold hairpin adorning her tresses.
Behind the warm lotus-flower curtain,
They took their pleasure in the spring night.

春宵苦短日高起①,从此君王不早朝②。
承欢侍宴无闲暇③,春从春游夜专夜④。
后宫佳丽三千人⑤,三千宠爱在一身⑥。
金屋妆成娇侍夜⑦,玉楼宴罢醉和春⑧。
姊妹弟兄皆列土⑨,可怜光彩生门户⑩。
遂令天下父母心⑪,不重生男重生女。
骊宫高处入青云⑫,仙乐风飘处处闻⑬。
缓歌慢舞凝丝竹⑭,尽日君王看不足。

①苦短:苦于春夜的时间太短。日高起:太阳升得老高才起来。

②不早朝:是说玄宗贪恋女色,不上早朝,不理政事。

③承欢:承受皇帝的欢爱。侍宴:陪伴玄宗宴饮。

④专夜:指杨贵妃夜夜得到玄宗的欢爱。

⑤后宫:义同“六宫”,后妃住处。

⑥在一身:集中在杨贵妃一人身上。

⑦金屋:指华丽的宫室。

⑧玉楼:华美的楼台。醉和春:即醉意和着春意。

⑨列土:分封领地。列,同裂。

⑩可怜:可爱,这里作可美解。

⑪遂令:就使得。

⑫骊宫:指骊山的华清宫。

⑬仙乐:指华清宫的美妙音乐声。

⑭“缓歌”句:是说轻慢的歌舞节拍与伴奏的音乐旋律极为吻合,凝合成了一个和谐的整体。丝,指弦乐器;竹,指管乐器。

Regretting only the spring nights were too short;
Rising only when the sun was high;
He stopped attending court sessions
In the early morning.
Constantly she amused and feasted with him,
Accompanying him on his spring outings,
Spending all the nights with him.
Though many beauties were in the palace,
More than three thousand of them,
All his favours were centred on her.
Finishing her coiffure in the gilded chamber,
Charming, she accompanied him at night.
Feasting together in the marble pavilion,
Inebriated in the spring.
All her sisters and brothers
Became nobles with fiefs.
How wonderful to have so much splendour
Centred in one family!
All parents wished for daughters
Instead of sons!
The Li Mountain lofty pleasure palace
Reached to the blue sky.
The sounds of heavenly music were carried
By the wind far and wide.
Gentle melodies and graceful dances
Mingled with the strings and flutes;
The emperor never tired of these.

①渔阳：唐代郡名,今河北省蓟县、平谷县一带。鞞(pí 皮)鼓：古代军中用的鼓,这里用以指战争。

②霓裳羽衣曲：唐代名曲,传为开元中西凉府节度使杨敬述所献的西域乐舞,初名《婆罗门曲》,后经唐玄宗润色,改名为《霓裳羽衣曲》。

③九重：指皇帝居住的地方。古代制度,皇宫由内到外有九道门,故称九重。城阙：指京城长安。烟尘生：指发生了战乱。

④西南行：向西南方前进,准备到四川去。

⑤翠华：指皇帝车驾上的旗帜,因是用翠鸟羽毛装饰的,故称翠华。行复止：指皇帝的车驾走走又停了下来。

⑥都门：都城的门,即长安西边的延秋门。百余里：指距离百余里的马嵬驿,故址在今陕西省兴平县西。

⑦六军：指给皇帝护驾的军队。不发：不肯前进。这句的意思是说,由于杨氏祸国,玄宗逃到马嵬驿时,护驾的将士不肯前进,龙武大将军陈玄礼发动兵变,杀了杨国忠等人,并逼着玄宗赐死杨妃。玄宗无可奈何,只得命高力士把杨妃缢死在佛堂。

⑧宛转：指杨妃临死时呻吟悱恻的样子。蛾眉：指美丽的女子,这里指杨妃。马前死：因当时形势

渔阳鞞鼓动地来①,惊破霓裳羽衣曲②。
九重城阙烟尘生③,千乘万骑西南行④。
翠华摇摇行复止⑤,西出都门百余里⑥。
六军不发无奈何⑦,宛转蛾眉马前死⑧。
花钿委地无人收⑨,翠翘金雀玉搔头⑩。
君王掩面救不得⑪,回看血泪相和流⑫。
黄埃散漫风萧索⑬,云栈萦纡登剑阁⑭。

紧迫,将士都骑在马上,所以说杨妃是"马前死"。

⑨花钿(diàn 店)：镶嵌花纹的首饰。委地：丢落在地上。

⑩翠翘：妇女的首饰。金雀：金钗名。玉搔头：玉制的簪子。

⑪君王：指唐玄宗。

⑫回看句：是写玄宗的伤痛,以至于血泪相和流。

⑬黄埃散漫：尘埃飞散。

⑭云栈：指高入云天的栈道。这是古代在险峻的山岩上用木头架设的通道,又称阁道。萦(yíng 营)纡(yū 迂)：回环曲折。剑阁：剑门山,在今四川省剑阁县北。

Then battle drums shook the earth,
The alarm sounding from Yuyang.
The Rainbow and Feather Garments Dance
Was stopped by sounds of war.
Dust filled the high-towered capital,
As thousands of carriages and horsemen
Fled to the southwest.
The emperor's green-canopied carriage
Was forced to halt,
Having left the west city gate
More than a hundred *li*.
There was nothing the emperor could do,
At the army's refusal to proceed.
So she with the moth-like eyebrows
Was killed before his horses.
Her floral-patterned gilded box
Fell to the ground, abandoned and unwanted,
Like her jade hairpin
With the gold sparrow and green feathers.
Covering his face with his hands,
He could not save her.
Turning back to look at her,
His tears mingled with her blood.
Yellow dust filled the sky;
The wind was cold and shrill.
Ascending high winding mountain paths,
They reached the Sword Pass,
At the foot of the Emei Mountains.

峨嵋山下少人行①,旌旗无光日色薄②。
蜀江水碧蜀山青③,圣主朝朝暮暮情④。
行宫见月伤心色⑤,夜雨闻铃肠断声⑥。
天旋地转回龙驭⑦,到此踌躇不能去⑧。
马嵬坡下泥土中⑨,不见玉颜空死处⑩。
君臣相顾尽沾衣,东望都门信马归⑪。
归来池苑皆依旧⑫,太液芙蓉未央柳⑬。

①峨嵋山:在今四川省峨嵋县境,成都市西南。

②旌旗:旗帜。日色薄:形容日光黯淡。

③蜀:蜀地,今四川省曾是古代蜀国的地方。

④圣主:指唐玄宗。

⑤行宫:皇帝临时的住地。

⑥铃:指行宫屋檐角上挂的铃铛。

⑦天旋地转:喻指时局发生重大变化。龙驭(yù 玉):皇帝的车驾。

⑧到此:指皇帝的车驾还京,来到了马嵬驿。不能去:不忍离去。

⑨马嵬坡:今陕西省兴平县西,即埋葬杨妃的地方。

⑩玉颜:美丽的容貌,此指杨妃。

⑪信马:随着马。

⑫池苑(yuàn 院):指宫中池子和园林。

⑬太液:太液池。汉代建章宫里的池名,在今陕西省西安市东。芙蓉:指水芙蓉,即荷花。未央:汉代宫名,故址在今西安市北。

Few came that way.
Their banners seemed less resplendent;
Even the sun seemed dim.
Though the rivers were deep blue,
And the Sichuan mountains green,
Night and day the emperor mourned.
In his refuge when he saw the moon,
Even it seemed sad and wan.
On rainy nights, the sound of bells
Seemed broken-hearted.
Fortunes changed, the emperor was restored.
His dragon-carriage started back.
Reaching the place where she died,
He lingered, reluctant to leave.
In the earth and dust of Mawei Slope,
No lady with the jade-like face was found.
The spot was desolate.
Emperor and servants exchanged looks,
Their clothes stained with tears.
Turning eastwards towards the capital,
They led their horses slowly back.
The palace was unchanged on his return,
With lotus blooming in the Taiye Pool
And willows in the Weiyang Palace.

①"芙蓉如面"句是说,看到池中艳丽的荷花,就象看到了杨妃的脸;看到了那秀美的柳叶,就象看到她的眉毛。

②对此:即对着"芙蓉如面柳如眉"的情景。

③西宫:即西内,指太极宫。南内:即兴庆宫,在宫城的南面,故称南内。

④红不扫:指秋天红叶落满庭阶也没人来扫去。

⑤梨园弟子:指玄宗当年在梨园训练的乐工。白发新:新添了白发。

⑥椒房:用花椒粉和泥涂壁,取其芳香,为后妃所住的宫室。阿监:宫中的女官。青娥:指宫女。

⑦夕殿:夜晚的宫殿。思悄然:意绪萧索,寂然无声。

⑧"孤灯"句:一个人不断地挑着孤灯,把灯芯都烧尽了,人还睡不着。

⑨钟鼓:宫中报时辰的。初长夜:秋夜更长了。

⑩耿耿:明亮。

⑪鸳鸯瓦:两片一俯一仰,嵌合成对的瓦。

⑫翡翠衾:上面绣有翡翠鸟的被子。

⑬悠悠:长远。经年:经过一年。

芙蓉如面柳如眉①,对此如何不泪垂②。
春风桃李花开日,秋雨梧桐叶落时。
西宫南内多秋草③,落叶满阶红不扫④。
梨园弟子白发新⑤,椒房阿监青娥老⑥。
夕殿萤飞思悄然⑦,孤灯挑尽未成眠⑧。
迟迟钟鼓初长夜⑨,耿耿星河欲曙天⑩。
鸳鸯瓦冷霜华重⑪,翡翠衾寒谁与共⑫。
悠悠生死别经年⑬,魂魄不曾来入梦。
临邛道士鸿都客⑭,能以精诚致魂魄⑮。

⑭临邛(qióng 穷):今四川省邛崃县。鸿都客:这是对从蜀地来的道士的美称。鸿都:东汉京城洛阳宫门名,是当时政府藏书的地方。

⑮精诚:真诚。这里是指道士的法术。致:招致,使来。

The lotus flowers were like her face;
The willows like her eyebrows.
How could he refrain from tears
At their sight?
The spring wind returned at night;
The peach and plum trees blossomed again.
Plane leaves fell in the autumn rains.
Weeds choked the emperor's west palace;
Piles of red leaves on the unswept steps.
The hair of the young musicians of the Pear Garden
Turned to grey.
The green-clad maids of the spiced chambers
Were growing old.
At night when glow-worms flitted in the pavilion
He thought of her in silence.
The lonely lamp was nearly extinguished,
Yet still he could not sleep.
The slow sound of bells and drums
Was heard in the long night.
The Milky Way glimmered bright.
It was almost dawn.
Cold and frosty the paired-love-bird tiles;
Chilly the kingfisher-feathered quilt
With none to share it.
Though she had died years before,
Her spirit never appeared even in his dreams.
A priest from Linqiong came to Chang'an,
Said to summon spirits at his will.

①展转思：翻来覆去的想念。

②殷勤觅：用心用意地寻找。

③排空驭气：腾云驾雾。

④之：指代杨妃。求之遍：到处去寻找她。

⑤碧落：道家称天为碧落。

⑥两处：即"碧落"和"黄泉"两处。

⑦仙山：指蓬莱山。

⑧五云：五色的云彩。

⑨绰约：轻盈柔美的样子。

⑩中有：指众仙中有。字太真：即杨妃。

⑪参(cēn)差(cī)是：仿佛就是。

⑫金阙：黄金作的宫阙。阙，门楼。玉扃(jiōng 駉)：玉作的门。

⑬小玉：战国时吴王夫差的女儿名小玉，这在唐代已成为婢女的通称。双成：姓董，传说中西王母的侍女。这里的小玉、双成都是借指为杨妃成仙后的侍女。

⑭汉家天子：借汉指唐，即唐玄宗李隆基。使：差来的人。

⑮九华帐：饰有繁丽花纹的帐子。

为感君王展转思①，遂教方士殷勤觅②。
排空驭气奔如电③，升天入地求之遍④。
上穷碧落下黄泉⑤，两处茫茫皆不见⑥。
忽闻海上有仙山⑦，山在虚无缥缈间。
楼阁玲珑五云起⑧，其中绰约多仙子⑨。
中有一人字太真⑩，雪肤花貌参差是⑪。
金阙西厢叩玉扃⑫，转教小玉报双成⑬。
闻道汉家天子使⑭，九华帐里梦魂惊⑮。

Moved by the emperor's longing for her,
He sent a magician to make a careful search.
Swift as lightning, through the air he sped,
Up to the heavens, below the earth, everywhere.
Though they searched the sky and nether regions,
Of her there was no sign.
Till he heard of a fairy mountain
In the ocean of a never-never land.
Ornate pavilions rose through coloured clouds,
Wherein dwelt lovely fairy folk.
One was named Taizhen,
With snowy skin and flowery beauty,
Suggesting that this might be she.
When he knocked at the jade door
Of the gilded palace's west chamber,
A fairy maid, Xiaoyu, answered,
Reporting to another, Shuangcheng.
On hearing of the messenger
From the Han emperor,
She was startled from her sleep
Behind the gorgeous curtain.

①揽衣：拿起衣服。

②珠箔（bó 泊）：珠帘。迤（yǐ 以）逦（lǐ 里）：曲折连绵的样子。

③云鬓半偏：因刚起床，尚未梳妆，头上的发鬓偏在一边。新睡觉：刚刚睡醒起来。

④袂（mèi 妹）：衣袖。

⑤犹似：还好象。连上两句是说，杨妃匆匆走下堂来，风吹起了衣袖，那飘飘欲飞的样子，还象当年演奏《霓裳羽衣曲》时那么轻盈柔美。

⑥玉容：美丽的容颜。阑干：纵横的样子。

⑦"梨花"句：比喻杨妃流泪时的动人形象。

⑧凝睇（dì 帝）：眼神注视。

⑨两渺茫：指玄宗与杨妃之间因长期隔绝而互相都不知道彼此的情况。

⑩昭阳殿：汉代宫殿名，为汉成帝刘骜的皇后赵飞燕住的地方，这里借指为杨妃生前所住的宫殿。

⑪蓬莱宫：仙人住的地方，这里是指杨妃死后所住的仙境。日月长：是说此后在蓬莱宫中的日子将是永久的了。

⑫人寰：人间世界。

⑬长安：唐代国都，皇帝住的地方，在今陕西省西安市。

揽衣推枕起徘徊①，珠箔银屏迤逦开②。
云鬓半偏新睡觉③，花冠不整下堂来。
风吹仙袂飘飘举④，犹似霓裳羽衣舞⑤。
玉容寂寞泪阑干⑥，梨花一枝春带雨⑦。
含情凝睇谢君王⑧，一别音容两渺茫⑨。
昭阳殿里恩爱绝⑩，蓬莱宫中日月长⑪。
回头下望人寰处⑫，不见长安见尘雾⑬。

Dressing, she drew it back,
Rising hesitantly.
The pearl curtains and silver screens
Opened in succession.
Her cloudy tresses were awry,
Just summoned from her sleep.
Without arranging her flower headdress,
She entered the hall.
The wind blew her fairy skirt,
Lifting it, as if she still danced
The Rainbow and Feather Garments Dance.
But her pale face was sad,
Tears filled her eyes,
Like a blossoming pear tree in spring,
With raindrops on its petals.
Controlling her feelings and looking away,
She thanked the emperor.
Since their parting she had not heard
His voice nor seen his face.
While she had been his first lady,
Their love had been ruptured.
Many years had passed
On Penglai fairy isle.
Turning her head,
She gazed down on the mortal world.
Chang'an could not be seen,
Only mist and dust.

惟将旧物表深情^①,钿合金钗寄将去^②。
钗留一股合一扇^③,钗擘黄金合分钿^④。
但教心似金钿坚,天上人间会相见。
临别殷勤重寄词^⑤,词中有誓两心知^⑥。
七月七日长生殿^⑦,夜半无人私语时^⑧。
在天愿作比翼鸟^⑨,在地愿为连理枝^⑩。
天长地久有时尽,此恨绵绵无绝期^⑪。

①惟将:只把。旧物:指生前玄宗给她的纪念物品,即下句所说的钿合、金钗。

②钿合:用黄金珠宝镶成花纹的盒子。

③"钗留"句:钗有两股,留下一股。钿合有两扇,留下一扇。

④擘(bò 簸):分开。

⑤重寄词:再三托使者寄语玄宗。

⑥两心知:指所说的誓词只有她和玄宗两人知道。

⑦长生殿:骊山华清宫里的殿堂。

⑧私语:两人私下说的话。

⑨比翼鸟:即鹣鹣(jiān 兼),传说是一种雌雄相爱,并翅而飞的鸟。

⑩连理枝:两树不同根而枝干却连结生长在一起,这也是古人用来象征爱情的。

⑪绵绵:永不断绝的样子。

She presented old mementos
To express her deep feeling.
Asking the messenger to take
The jewel box and the golden pin.
"I'll keep one half of the pin and box;
Breaking the golden pin
And keeping the jewel lid.
As long as our love lasts
Like jewels and gold,
We may meet again
In heaven or on earth."
Before they parted
She again sent this message,
Containing a pledge
Only she and the emperor knew.
In the Palace of Eternal Youth
On the seventh of the seventh moon,
Alone they had whispered
To each other at midnight:
"In heaven we shall be birds
Flying side by side.
On earth flowering sprigs
On the same branch!"
Heaven and earth may not last for ever,
But this sorrow was eternal.

此诗为《长恨歌》的姊妹篇,是白居易著名的叙事长诗。由记叙琵琶女的身世飘零,感叹自身的宦途潦倒。"同是天涯沦落人,相逢何必曾相识"则深沉地唱出了对人生的无限感慨。本诗流传很广,影响至深。元代马致远据此创作《青衫泪》杂剧。

元和十年,余左迁九江郡司马①。明年秋,送客湓浦口,闻舟中夜弹琵琶者,听其音,铮铮然有京都声②。问其人,本长安倡女,尝学琵琶于穆、曹二善才,年长色衰,委身为贾人妇③。遂命酒,使快弹数曲;曲罢悯然④。自叙少小时欢乐事,今漂沦憔悴,转徙于江湖间⑤。余出官二年,恬然自安,感斯人言,是夕始觉有迁谪意⑥。因为长句,歌以赠之,凡六百一十二言,命曰《琵琶行》⑦。

浔阳江头夜送客,枫叶荻花秋瑟瑟⑧。
主人下马客在船,举酒欲饮无管弦⑨。
醉不成欢惨将别,别时茫茫江浸月。
忽闻水上琵琶声,主人忘归客不发。
寻声暗问弹者谁? 琵琶声停欲语迟。
移船相近邀相见,添酒回灯重开宴⑩。

①元和:唐宪宗李纯的年号。元和十年:即公元 815 年。左迁:降职。九江郡:原是隋朝的郡名,唐改为江州,州治在今江西省九江市。下文"浔阳城"、"江州"均指九江一地。司马:官名,州刺史下面管军事的副职。

②湓(pén 盆)浦口:湓水流入长江的地方,在九江城西。铮(zhēng 争)铮:象声词,形容琵琶弹奏发出的音响。

③善才:唐代对琵琶艺人或曲师的通称。委身:将自身托付给别人。贾(gǔ 古)人:商人。

④命酒:吩咐摆酒。悯:忧愁。

⑤漂沦:漂泊,沉沦,很不得意。转徙:辗转迁徙。

⑥自安:自以为安适。迁谪意:被贬谪的不愉快的心情。

⑦凡:共。言:字。六百一十二言:不确,全诗为八十八句,六百一十六言。

⑧浔阳江:指长江流经九江这一段的别名。瑟瑟:秋风吹动枫叶、荻花发出的声音。

⑨主人下马客在船:是说作者下马到客人所在的船中送别客人。

⑩回灯:把灯拨得更亮。

In AD 815, the tenth year of the reign of Yuanhe, I was demoted to the assistant prefectship of Jiujiang. The next autumn, while seeing a friend off at Pengpu, I heard someone strumming a lute in a boat at night, playing with the touch of a musician from the capital. I found upon inquiry that the lutist was a courtesan from Chang'an who had learned from the musicians Mu and Cao but growing old and losing her looks, she had married a merchant. Then I ordered drinks and asked her to play a few tunes. After playing, in deep distress, she told me of the pleasures of her youth and said now that her beauty had faded she was drifting from place to place by rivers and lakes. In my two years as an official away from the capital I had been resigned enough, my mind at peace, but moved by her tale that night I began to take my demotion and exile to heart. So I wrote a long poem and presented it to her. It has 612 words and I call it the Song of the Lute Player.

By the Xunyang River a guest is seen off one night;
Chill the autumn, red the maple leaves and in flower the reeds;
The host alights from his horse, the guest is aboard,
They raise their cups to drink but have no music.
Drunk without joy, in sadness they must part;
At the time of parting the river seems steeped in moonlight;
Suddenly out on the water a lute is heard;
The host forgets to turn back, the guest delays going.
Seeking the sound in the dark, we ask who is the player.
The lute is silent; hesitant the reply.
Rowing closer, we ask if we may meet the musician,
Call for more wine, trim the lamp and resume our feast;

①转轴：拧转琵琶上的弦轴，以调音定调。

②掩抑：指声调低沉。思（si四）：悲。

③信手：随手。

④拢、捻、抹、挑：指弹琵琶的各种不同的指法。《霓裳》、《六幺》：均为曲调名。

⑤大弦：粗弦即低音弦。嘈嘈：形容声音沉重舒长。小弦：细弦即高音弦。切切：形容声音急促细碎。

⑥间关：鸟声。这句形容乐声象黄莺的叫声在花底流过。冰下难：这是形容乐声象冰下流动的泉水，幽咽难鸣。

⑦冰泉冷涩：形容乐声象结冰的泉水那样清冷凝涩。弦凝绝：弦声凝滞停顿。

⑧"银瓶"两句是说，乐声象银瓶忽然破裂，水浆逆射；又象铁骑突出，刀枪齐鸣。这是形容乐声在稍停之后，忽又高扬起来。

⑨拨：弹琵琶的拨片。画：同"划"。当心画：用拨子从琵琶中部划过四弦，一般表示曲终。四弦一声：四根弦同时发声。

⑩舫（fǎng访）：船。

千呼万唤始出来，犹抱琵琶半遮面。
转轴拨弦三两声，未成曲调先有情①。
弦弦掩抑声声思，似诉平生不得志②。
低眉信手续续弹，说尽心中无限事③。
轻拢慢捻抹复挑，初为《霓裳》后《六幺》④。
大弦嘈嘈如急雨，小弦切切如私语⑤。
嘈嘈切切错杂弹，大珠小珠落玉盘。
间关莺语花底滑，幽咽泉流冰下难⑥。
冰泉冷涩弦凝绝，凝绝不通声渐歇⑦。
别有幽愁暗恨生，此时无声胜有声。
银瓶乍破水浆迸，铁骑突出刀枪鸣⑧。
曲终收拨当心画，四弦一声如裂帛⑨。
东舟西舫悄无言，唯见江心秋月白⑩。

Only after a thousand entreaties does she appear,
Her face half-hidden behind the lute in her arms.
She tunes up and plucks the strings a few times,
Touching our hearts before even the tune is played;
Each chord strikes a pensive note
As if voicing the disillusion of a lifetime;
Her head is bent, her fingers stray over the strings
Pouring out the infinite sorrows of her heart.
Lightly she pinches in the strings, slowly she strums and plucks
    them;
First *The Rainbow Garments*, then *The Six Minor Notes*.
The high notes wail like pelting rain,
The low notes whisper like soft confidences;
Wailing and whispering interweave
Like pearls large and small cascading on a plate of jade,
Like a warbling oriole gliding below the blossom,
Like a mountain brook purling down a bank,
Till the brook turns to ice, the strings seem about to snap,
About to snap, and for one instant all is still
Only an undertone of quiet grief
Is more poignant in the silence than any sound;
Then a silver bottle is smashed, out gushes the water,
Armoured riders charge, their swords and lances clang!
When the tune ends, she draws her pick full across
And the four strings give a sound like the tearing of silk.
Right and left of the boat all is silence —
We see only the autumn moon, silver in midstream.

185

①敛容:对客人矜持而有礼貌的样子。

②虾蟆陵:即下马陵,在唐代长安城东南曲江附近。

③教坊:唐代官办的教习歌舞技艺的机构。

④秋娘:当时长安著名的乐伎。

⑤五陵:长安城外地名,该处有汉高帝长陵,唐代安陵,景帝阳陵,武帝茂陵和昭帝平陵。五陵年少:泛指当时达官贵人家的子弟。缠头:赠给歌舞女子的贵重丝织品,叫做缠头。绡:生丝制成的纺织品。

⑥钿(diàn店)头云篦:两头饰有花钿的发篦。击节:打拍子。翻酒污:是说被同少年们戏谑时打翻的杯酒弄脏。

⑦秋月春风:这里指青春岁月。等闲度:随便打发过去了。

⑧阿姨:教坊中管歌女的头目。颜色故:容颜衰减。

⑨浮梁:唐县名,即今江西景德镇市。

⑩去来:自商人去浮梁以来。

⑪妆泪:眼泪与脸上的脂粉相混。红:指脸上的胭脂色。阑干:泪流纵横的样子。

⑫重:更加。唧唧:叹息声。

沉吟放拨插弦中,整顿衣裳起敛容①。
自言本是京城女,家在虾蟆陵下住②。
十三学得琵琶成,名属教坊第一部③。
曲罢曾教善才伏,妆成每被秋娘妒④。
五陵年少争缠头,一曲红绡不知数⑤。
钿头云篦击节碎,血色罗裙翻酒污⑥。
今年欢笑复明年,秋月春风等闲度⑦。
弟走从军阿姨死,暮去朝来颜色故⑧。
门前冷落车马稀,老大嫁作商人妇。
商人重利轻别离,前月浮梁买茶去⑨。
去来江口守空船,绕船月明江水寒⑩。
夜深忽梦少年事,梦啼妆泪红阑干⑪。
我闻琵琶已叹息,又闻此语重唧唧⑫。
同是天涯沦落人,相逢何必曾相识!

Pensively she puts the pick between the strings,
Straightens her clothes, rises and composes herself.
She is, she says, a girl from the capital
Whose family once lived at the foot of Toad Hill.
At thirteen she learned to play the lute
And ranked first among the musicians;
Her playing was admired by the old masters,
Her looks were the envy of other courtesans;
Youths from wealthy districts vied in their gifts to engage her,
A single song brought her countless rolls of red silk;
Men smashed jewelled and silver trinkets to mark the beat;
Silk skirts as red as blood were stained by spilt wine.
Pleasure and laughter from one year to the next,
While the autumn moon and spring breeze passed unheeded.
Then her brother joined the army, her aunt died,
The days and nights slipped by and her beauty faded,
No more carriages and horsemen thronged her gate,
And growing old she became a merchant's wife.
The merchant thought only of profit: to seek it he leaves her.
Two months ago he went to Fuliang to buy tea,
Leaving her alone in the boat at the mouth of the river;
All around the moonlight is bright, the river is cold,
And late at night, dreaming of her girlhood,
She cries in her sleep, staining her rouged cheeks with tears.
The music of her lute has made me sigh,
And now she tells this plaintive tale of sorrow;
We are both ill-starred, drifting on the face of the earth;
No matter if we were strangers before this encounter.

我从去年辞帝京,谪居卧病浔阳城①。
浔阳地僻无音乐,终岁不闻丝竹声②。
住近湓江地低湿,黄芦苦竹绕宅生。
其间旦暮闻何物?杜鹃啼血猿哀鸣③。
春江花朝秋月夜,往往取酒还独倾。
岂无山歌与村笛?呕哑嘲哳难为听④。
今夜闻君琵琶语,如听仙乐耳暂明⑤。
莫辞更坐弹一曲,为君翻作琵琶行⑥。
感我此言良久立,却坐促弦弦转急⑦。
凄凄不似向前声,满座重闻皆掩泣⑧。
座中泣下谁最多?江州司马青衫湿⑨。

①帝京:指长安。

②浔阳:浔阳城,今江西九江市。

③杜鹃啼血:相传杜鹃鸟悲啼时,嘴里会流出血来。

④呕哑嘲哳(zhā zhā):都是象声词,指嘈杂难听的声音。

⑤琵琶语:琵琶乐声。

⑥更坐:重新坐下。翻作:依曲调翻成歌词。

⑦却坐:回到原来的位置坐下。促弦:把弦调紧。

⑧向前:刚才。

⑨青衫:黑色的官服,唐代低级官员(八品、九品)穿的。

Last year I bade the imperial city farewell;

A demoted official, I lay ill in Xunyang;

Xunyang is a paltry place without any music,

For one year I heard no wind instruments, no strings.

Now I live on the low, damp flat by the River Peng,

Round my house yellow reeds and bitter bamboos grow rife;

From dawn till dusk I hear no other sounds

But the wailing of night-jars and the moaning of apes.

On a day of spring blossoms by the river or moonlit night in autumn

I often call for wine and drink alone;

Of course, there are rustic songs and village pipes,

But their shrill discordant notes grate on my ears;

Tonight listening to your lute playing

Was like hearing fairy music; it gladdened my ears.

Don 't refuse, but sit down and play another tune,

And I'll write a *Song of the Lute Player* for you.

Touched by my words, she stands there for some time,

Then goes back to her seat and plays with quickened tempo

Music sadder far than the first melody,

And at the sound not a man of us has dry eyes.

The assistant prefect of Jiangzhou is so moved

That his blue coat is wet with tears.

钱塘湖春行·白居易(772—846)

诗人以移步换景的写法,在行进中摄取最富春天气息的镜头,从水、云、早莺、新燕、乱花、浅草等不同角度,饱含深情地刻画西湖春景和自然界的勃勃生机。语言平实精纯、宛转流畅,全无斧凿之痕。

"钱塘湖"即今杭州西湖。

孤山寺北贾亭西,水面初平云脚低①。
几处早莺争暖树,谁家新燕啄春泥②。
乱花渐欲迷人眼,浅草才能没马蹄③。
最爱湖东行不足,绿杨阴里白沙堤④。

①孤山:在今杭州西湖中后湖与外湖之间,山上有孤山寺。贾亭:杭州刺史贾全于钱塘湖建亭,名贾公亭。水面初平:指春天湖水上涨,水平齐岸。云脚:雨前或雨后接近地面的云气叫做"云脚"。

②争暖树:争着飞向向阳的树。啄:衔。

③乱:繁、多的意思。

④行不足:游赏得还不够。白沙堤:又名十锦塘,即今杭州西湖白堤。

190

North of Gushan Monastery, west of the Jia Pavilion,
Water brims level with the bank, the clouds hang low;
Here and there, the first orioles are disputing for sunny trees,
Young swallows, just down from the eaves, peck in the spring
   mud.
The riot of flowers begins to dazzle the eye,
The short grass barely covers the horses' hooves;
I love best the east of the lake, and could stroll forever
On that white-sand embankment shaded by green willows.

雁门太守行·李贺（790—816）

诗人借用乐府古题,描写了元和年间在易水一带进行的平叛战争。全诗运用色彩浓重的语言,构成一幅有声、有色、有动、有静的战斗画面,增强了诗歌的表现力,反映了诗人要求削平藩镇,实现国家统一的思想。

"雁门"是郡名,在今山西省大同市东北一带。

黑云压城城欲摧,甲光向日金鳞开①。
角声满天秋色里,塞上燕脂凝夜紫②。
半卷红旗临易水,霜重鼓寒声不起③。
报君黄金台上意,提携玉龙为君死④。

①黑云压城:形容战争形势很紧张。甲光:指铠甲迎着太阳发出的闪光。金鳞:是说像金色的鱼鳞。

②燕脂:同"胭脂"。这里形容边塞土地的颜色。

③半卷红旗:指行军途中风力大,因而卷起红旗,减少阻力。易水:源出河北省易县。声不起:指鼓声低沉。

④黄金台上意:指君王的深恩厚意。黄金台,战国时燕昭王所筑,故址在今河北省易县东南。据说台上放置千金,以招揽人才。提携:拿起。玉龙:指宝剑。

Black clouds bear down upon the tottering town,
Armour glints like golden fish-scales in the sun,
Bugling invests the sky with autumn splendour
As crimson forts freeze in the purple dusk;
Red flags half-furled withdraw to the River Yi,
Our drums roll faint, muffled in heavy frost,
And to repay honour conferred from the golden dais, ①
I draw my Jade Dragon Sword to die for my lord!

---

① The dais from which the governor received his appointment from the emperor.

本诗用拟人手法，赋予铜人以丰富的想象，构成了一个完整的艺术形象，抒发了诗人对革新派人士不幸遭遇的深切同情，对唐帝国的日益衰微的无限感叹。

汉武帝曾在长安建造神明台，上铸铜仙人以掌托铜盘盛露，取露和玉屑，饮以求仙。

魏明帝青龙元年八月，诏宫官牵车西取汉孝武捧露盘仙人，欲立置前殿①。宫官既拆盘，仙人临载，乃潸然泪下②。唐诸王孙李长吉遂作《金铜仙人辞汉歌》③。

茂陵刘郎秋风客，夜闻马嘶晓无迹④。
画栏桂树悬秋香，三十六宫土花碧⑤。
魏官牵车指千里，东关酸风射眸子⑥。
空将汉月出宫门，忆君清泪如铅水⑦。
衰兰送客咸阳道，天若有情天亦老⑧。
携盘独出月荒凉，渭城已远波声小⑨。

①青龙：是魏明帝曹睿（ruì锐）的一个年号。青龙元年：据《魏略》应为魏明帝景初元年（237）。诏：诏令，皇帝的命令。西取：魏建都洛阳，西汉建都长安，在洛阳西，魏明帝派官到长安拆运铜人，所以说"西取"。汉孝武：即汉武帝刘彻。前殿：殿前。

②临载：当起运时。潸（shān山）然：涕泪下流的样子。

③唐诸王孙李长吉：李贺是唐宗室郑王的后代，故自称"唐诸王孙"。

④茂陵：汉武帝墓，在今陕西省兴平县。刘郎：指汉武帝。秋风客：汉武帝曾作《秋风辞》，以此称他。

⑤画栏：指汉武帝宫殿里彩绘的栏杆。秋香：指桂花。三十六宫：汉代长安离宫有三十六所。土花：苔藓。

⑥指：直指，直往。东关：函谷关。酸风：凄凉的风。眸（móu谋）子：眼中的瞳人。

⑦将：共，与。君：指汉武帝。

⑧客：指金铜仙人。咸阳：秦代都城，旧址在今陕西省咸阳市东，这里借指长安。咸阳道：当时由长安至洛阳的通道。

⑨盘：指金铜仙人所携之承露盘。渭城：即秦咸阳，这里借指长安。

In the eighth month of the first year of the Qinglong era, during the reign of Emperor Ming of Wei, the court ordered a palace officer to ride west and bring back the gilded bronze figure of an immortal holding a disc to catch dew made during the reign of Emperor Wu of Han, in order to set it up in the front court. When the palace officer removed the disc and took the statue to his carriage, the bronze figure shed tears. So Li Changji, descended from a prince of the House of Tang, wrote this song.

Gone that emperor of Maoling,
Rider through the autumn wind,
Whose horse neighs at night
And has passed without trace by dawn.
The fragrance of autumn lingers still
On those cassia trees by painted galleries,
But on every palace hall the green moss grows.
As Wei's envoy sets out to drive a thousand *li*
The keen wind at the East Gate stings the statue's eyes...
From the ruined palace he brings nothing forth
But the moon-shaped disc of Han,
True to his lord, he sheds leaden tears,
And withered orchids by the Xianyang Road
See the traveller on his way.
Ah, if Heaven had a feeling heart, it too must grow old!
He bears the disc off alone
By the light of a desolate moon,
The town far behind him, muted its lapping waves.

杜牧的绝句具有很高的艺术成就,最为后人激赏。本诗前两句以绚烂的色彩,描绘出江南生机勃勃、莺鸣花放的春景,极富诗情画意。后两句寓抒怀于写景之中,表达了诗人对朝代兴亡的感慨。全诗语句清新明畅,脍炙人口,令人品味无穷。

千里莺啼绿映红,
水村山郭酒旗风。
南朝四百八十寺①,
多少楼台烟雨中②。

①南朝:宋、齐、梁、陈四朝。
②四百八十寺:南朝帝王贵族多好佛,据说建有五百多座寺院,拥有僧尼十余万。

Orioles can be heard singing amid the red and green for a thousand *li* ,
And wineshop streamers flutter in lakeside villages and hillside towns.
Of the 480 temples built by the Southern Dynasties, ①
Many towers and terraces still remain erect in the misty rain.

---

① Most emperors of the Southern Dynasties (AD 420-589) are known for their
devout Buddhism, and had a great number of Buddhist monasteries built all over South
China.

杜牧的写景小诗词句翩翩,写得历历如画,思致活泼,富有爽朗向上的激情,具有清新飘逸的独特风格。本诗把山中秋景写得色彩绚艳,形象鲜明,而富于生机。其中"霜叶红于二月花"明朗而又含蓄,读后给人以清新愉悦的美感,因而成为历代传诵之名句。

远上寒山石径斜①,
白云生处有人家②。
停车坐爱枫林晚③,
霜叶红于二月花。

① 寒山:深秋时节的山。

② 白云生处:指山林的最深处,远望白云层生。

③ 坐:因。晚:夕阳晚照。

A flag-stone path winds up into the chilly hills,
Where houses are just discernible amid the thick white cloud.
I stop my carriage for I love the maple trees in the twilight,
The leaves after early frost are as crimson as spring flowers.

词产生于民间,最初不过是民间俚曲。盛唐时出现文人词,晚唐温庭筠是第一位专力于"倚声填词"的作家。他的词多写花间月下、闺情绮怨,形成了以绮艳香软为特征的花间词风,被称为"花间鼻祖",也是中国文人词的主要奠基人之一。

小山重叠金明灭①,鬓云欲度香腮雪②。懒起画蛾眉③,弄妆梳洗迟。

照花前后镜④,花面交相映。新帖绣罗襦⑤,双双金鹧鸪⑥。

①小山:指屏山,即屏风。金明灭:屏风上彩绘闪烁的样子。

②鬓云:鬓发。度:遮住。雪:言皮肤之白。

③蛾眉:本指蚕蛾的触角,细长而弯曲,常用以比喻美人的眉毛。

④"照花"句:用两面镜子,一前一后照头上所插戴的花。

⑤"新帖"句:锦绣罗袄上,又绣贴了新图案。帖:即贴。襦(rú儒):短袄。

⑥金鹧鸪:指新贴绣在罗襦上的金线绣的鹧鸪鸟图案。

Dwarfish mountains, fold upon fold,
Embers of the day's dying gold.
Cloudy tresses softly lean
On spicy cheeks of snowy sheen;
While languid still she doth recline
To paint her moth-like eyebrows fine;
Then idly with her trinkets plays,
And to adorn herself delays.
Through inverted glass she peeps
Where in her hair a blossom sleeps,
While blossom fair and countenance
Do each the other's grace enhance.
Her new silk gown, embroidered rare,
Shows golden cuckoos pair by pair.

温词题材狭窄,风格不离红香翠软,因而被人讽为"男子而作闺音"。而本词却是温词中别具一格的清新自然之作。明显受到民间曲子词的影响,以白描手法刻画一位思妇在江楼期盼丈夫归来的图景。风格淡雅,语短情长。

梳洗罢,独倚望江楼。过尽千帆皆不是,斜晖脉脉水悠悠①,肠断白蘋洲②。

①斜晖:西斜的阳光。脉脉:含情相视的样子。

②白蘋洲:长满蘋草的水洲。蘋花色白,故云白蘋。

The damsel now herself arrays;
By river-tow'r alone she stays,
And sees a thousand sails pass by;
Her lover's boat she cannot spy.
The setting sun in twilight glows,
The tranquil river rippling flows;
Beside the isle, no sight of him,
She gazes at the duckweed white.

李商隐的代表作。本诗为诗人因聆听弹瑟而升起的对往事的追忆与感伤。诗中并未明确回忆往事,只是在中间四句朦胧地表达了对过去岁月的惆怅和沉痛。在写法上,用了一连串的意象比喻,使锦瑟音乐成为追忆往事的媒介物。全诗以锦瑟关合。

锦瑟无端五十弦,一弦一柱思华年①。
庄生晓梦迷蝴蝶,望帝春心托杜鹃②。
沧海月明珠有泪,蓝田日暖玉生烟③。
此情可待成追忆,只是当时已惘然④。

① 锦瑟:彩绘如锦绣一般华美的瑟。瑟:一种弦乐器。无端:无缘无故地,不知为什么。柱:系弦的支柱,每弦一柱。

② 庄生:指庄周。晓梦:梦醒了。迷蝴蝶:为蝴蝶梦所迷惑。《庄子·齐物论》说:一次庄子梦见自己化为蝴蝶,觉得自己就是真蝴蝶了,便不知自己是庄子。不久梦醒过来,又觉得自己真是庄子,而不是蝴蝶。望帝:传说中的古蜀国的一个君主的称号,名杜宇,死后魂魄化为杜鹃鸟,啼声哀切。春心:伤春的情思。指望帝失国的悲痛。托杜鹃:是说望帝把他的悲痛寄托在杜鹃哀切的啼声中。

③ 珠有泪:《博物志》说,南海之外,有鲛人,他哭泣时流下的眼泪,就是亮晶晶的珠子。 蓝田:即蓝田山,在今陕西省蓝田县,因山上产玉,又名玉山。玉生烟:指在阳光照耀下玉山所散发出的烟霭。这两句以"沧海月明"、"蓝田日暖"比喻自己所追求的美好理想,以"珠有泪"、"玉生烟"比喻理想的幻灭。意思是说,美好的理想,像鲛人的泪珠洒落海中,终成泡影;像玉山上升起的烟霭,随风飘散。

④ 此情:指以上四句所说的情景。可待:岂待。惘然:怅惘失意的样子。

For no reason the gorgeous zither has fifty strings,
Each string, each fret, recalls a youthful year.
Master Zhuang woke from a dream puzzled by a butterfly,[①]
Emperor Wang reposed his amorous heart to the cuckoo.[②]
The moon shines on the sea, pearls look like tears,
The sun is warm at Lantian,[③] the jade emits mist.
This feeling might have become a memory to recall,
But, even then, it was already suggestive of sorrows.

① According to a fabled story, Zhuang Zi (c. 369-286 BC), a famous philosopher of the Warring States Period, dreamt of being a butterfly and when he woke up, he was so confused that he could not tell whether it was him that had dreamt of being a butterfly or it was a butterfly that was then dreaming of being him.

② A legendary king who had an affair with his prime minister's wife and after his death his spirit changed into the cuckoo.

③ A hill famous for its jade in present-day Lantian County, Shaanxi Province.

这首咏蝉诗构思精巧。诗人抓住蝉的特点,结合自己的情思,"为情而造文",有所寄托。首句闻蝉鸣而起兴,末联又回到咏蝉上来,用拟人手法写蝉。"君"与"我"对举,咏物与抒情紧密结合,而又呼应开头,首尾圆合。

本以高难饱,　徒劳恨费声①。
五更疏欲断,　一树碧无情②。
薄宦梗犹泛,　故园芜已平③。
烦君最相警,　我亦举家清④。

①以高难饱:古人认为蝉栖高树,是餐风饮露的,因此把蝉当作高洁的象征。这句是说,既栖高树,自然是难以饱腹的。这里的"高"字,意义双关,既指蝉的高栖,又指蝉的高洁。费声:枉费鸣声。

②疏欲断:是说蝉长夜悲鸣,到天亮时,已力竭声嘶,稀疏到要断绝了。碧无情:是说蝉哀鸣树上,而树色依然如故,毫不动情。

③薄宦:卑微的官职。梗犹泛:喻指行踪飘泊不定。梗,树枝。泛,漂浮。芜已平:是说丛生的杂草,快要把故园平没了。

④烦:劳,麻烦。君:指蝉。最相警:最能使人警觉。举家清:全家清苦。

Existing on your high place, your belly can hardly be full,
All in vain is your resentful shrill.
At dawn the intermittent cry is about to cease,
But the tree remains indifferently green.
A peach-wood idol adrift,[①] to the court a petty servant,
My garden by weeds is overrun.
Much I'm obliged to you for your admonition,
I too, with my family, live in dire want.

---

①   The allusion is taken from a fabled dialogue between a peach-wood idol and a clay idol, which reflects their respective helpless situation in the coming rainfall and flood.

李商隐写了不少《无题》诗,本诗便是其中一首代表作,写他爱情生活的一个片断。这首诗写微妙的爱情心理,采用暗示的方法,如以"彩凤双飞"暗示男女的爱情结合,以"心有灵犀一点通"暗示两情相悦、两心相许,优美含蓄,是古代情诗中的杰作。

昨夜星辰昨夜风,画楼西畔桂堂东①。
身无彩凤双飞翼,心有灵犀一点通②。
隔座送钩春酒暖,分曹射覆蜡灯红③。
嗟余听鼓应官去,走马兰台类转蓬④。

①画楼:彩绘华丽的高楼。桂堂:形容厅堂芳美。

②灵犀:指犀牛角。传说犀牛是灵异之兽,角上有条白纹,从角端直通大脑,感应灵敏,所以称灵犀。这里借喻彼此心意相通。

③送钩:将钩藏于手中叫人猜的游戏。分曹:分队。射覆:把东西覆盖在器皿下叫人猜,也是古代的一种游戏。

④鼓:报晓的更鼓。兰台:唐高宗龙朔初年,改称秘书省为兰台。类:似。

The stars of last night, the breeze of last night,
West of the Painted Bower, east of the Osmanthus Hall.
We can't fly wing to wing like a pair of phoenixes,
Yet our hearts closely linked beat in harmony.
Maybe you're gaming over a cup of warm spring wine,
Or perhaps betting with friends in the red candlelight.
Alas! The drumbeat at dawn calls me to my duties,
I must ride to the Royal Secretariat like a tumbleweed adrift.

虞美人(春花秋月何时了)·李煜(937—978)

本诗是李煜作为亡国之君写下的著名词作。作者在词中抒发了自己的亡国之恨、故国之思。据说,此词一出,大街小巷竞相传唱,宋太宗闻之,以为"故国不堪回首月明中"暗含复国之心,于是不久即赐药酒将李后主毒死,此词由此成为李煜的绝命词。

春花秋月何时了?往事知多少!小楼昨夜又东风①,故国不堪回首月明中②。

雕栏玉砌应犹在③,只是朱颜改④。问君能有几多愁⑤?恰似一江春水向东流。

①又东风:又刮起了东风,意即春天又到了。

②故国:指南唐故都金陵。

③雕栏玉砌:雕花的栏杆和白玉石砌的台阶。这里代指南唐皇宫的建筑。应犹在:应该还在吧?

④朱颜改:红润的脸色变得憔悴了。这里指南唐宫女变得衰老憔悴了。

⑤问君:作者设问,实则自问之词。

There is no end to moonlit autumns or flowery springs,
And I have known so very many things.
From my turret the wind was in the east again last night.
A lost land was too much to bear: I turned from the moonlight.

The carven rail and jadework wall are as they were before:
Those rosy cheeks alone are there no more.
Tell me, what is the uttermost extent of pain, you say?
Mine is a river swollen in spring and welling east away.

晚唐五代的文人词多为应歌而作,供娱宾遣兴之用,内容亦未脱"词为艳科"的樊篱。李煜打破了这一传统,以词抒写性灵,使词"眼界始大,感慨遂深,遂变伶工之词而为士大夫之词"(王国维《人间词话》)。

帘外雨潺潺①,春意阑珊②,罗衾不耐五更寒③。梦里不知身是客④,一晌贪欢⑤。

独自莫凭栏⑥,无限江山⑦,别时容易见时难。流水落花春去也⑧,天上人间⑨。

①潺(chán 蝉)潺:雨声。

②阑珊:衰残,将尽。

③罗衾(qīn 钦):丝绸做的被子。

④身是客:指作者身为俘虏,远离故国。

⑤一晌:一会儿,片刻。

⑥凭栏:指倚栏远望。

⑦无限江山:指无限美好的南唐江山。

⑧"流水"句:落花随流水而去,春天已经完了。

⑨天上人间:意谓难以寻觅,变化之大有天壤之别。

Without the blind the rain is pattering,
Last intimation of the spring.
These gauzy coverlets too little warmth at midnight bring
To one who in his dreams fancied he was his own once more,
Once fed and avid for the thing.

I'd lean upon the rail, but what's the worth?
Of hills to cross there is no dearth.
Visions of what I left so lightly bring me no more mirth
Than fallen flowers faring home upon a running stream.
Heaven is high, and man is on earth.

这首词是柳永羁旅行役词的代表作，充分体现了柳词婉约的风格。据载，苏轼曾问手下："我词何如柳七？"手下回答："柳郎中词，只合十七八女郎，执红牙板，歌'杨柳岸、晓风残月'。学士词，须关西大汉，铜琵琶，铁绰板，唱'大江东去'"。

①长亭：古代路旁设有亭舍，供人休息用，常作送别饯行的地方。

②初歇：刚止。

③都门：京城，此指宋都汴京（即今河南省开封市）郊外。帐饮：指送别宴。无绪：无心思。

④处：指时候。

⑤兰舟：木兰树做的船，此指华美的船。

⑥凝噎(yè 业)：即凝咽，气咽声堵，悲伤得说不出话来。

⑦念：想到。去去：不断前行，即远去。

⑧楚天：泛指南方的天空。

⑨清秋节：凄清的秋季。

⑩经年：年复一年。

⑪风情：风月情怀，即男女恋情。

寒蝉凄切，对长亭晚①，骤雨初歇②。都门帐饮无绪③，留恋处④，兰舟催发⑤。执手相看泪眼，竟无语凝噎⑥。念去去、千里烟波⑦，暮霭沉沉楚天阔⑧。

多情自古伤离别，更那堪、冷落清秋节⑨！今宵酒醒何处？杨柳岸、晓风残月。此去经年⑩，应是良辰好景虚设。便纵有千种风情⑪，更与何人说！

Mournfully chirr the cicadas,
As the shower of rain stops
And we face the roadside pavilion at dusk.
We drink without cheer in the tent outside the city gate;
It is the moment when we are loath to part
But the magnolia-wood boat beckons me on.
Hands clasped together we see our tears,
So overcome, unable to utter a single word.
Ahead lies a journey a thousand *li* of misty waves
And the vast sky of Chu① hangs with heavy evening haze.

Since time immemorial, lovers have grieved at parting
Made more poignant in the fallow season of autumn.
What is this place where I have sobered from my drunken stupor?
"The riverside is strewn with willow trees,
The morning breeze wafts in with a waning moon."②
Our parting will last for years,
Fine hours and scenes of beauty have no appeal
Even though my heart is filled with tender feelings,
But, with whom can I share them?

_____

① Referring to the region of the ancient State of Chu situated in the central and southeast part of the country.

② A scene the poet imagines might occur on his journey.

唐五代至宋初,文人词体调多为小令,篇幅短小,无法表达广阔的内容。柳永创制了大量长调慢词,丰富了词的容量,促进了慢词的兴盛。本词便是他的慢词代表作,据说,金主完颜亮正是闻此词后,才起渡江之志的。

①形胜:地理形势优越。

②三吴:吴兴(在今浙江省)、吴郡(今江苏省苏州市)、会稽(今浙江省绍兴市)世称三吴。

③风帘:挡风的帘子。

④云树:树木很多,相连如云。

⑤天堑:天然的壕堑,此指钱塘江。

⑥玑:不圆的珠子。

⑦户盈罗绮(qǐ 起):家家户户穿的是绫罗绸缎。

⑧重湖:西湖分外湖、里湖,故称重湖。 叠巘(yǎn 演):重叠的山峦。

⑨三秋:秋季三个月中的第三个月,即阴历九月。

⑩羌管:笛子为羌人所制,故称笛子为羌管,这里泛指乐器。

⑪泛夜:夜间在水上浮动。

⑫莲娃:采莲女子。

东南形胜①,三吴都会②,钱塘自古繁华。烟柳画桥,风帘翠幕③,参差十万人家。云树绕堤沙④,怒涛卷霜雪,天堑无涯⑤。市列珠玑⑥,户盈罗绮⑦,竞豪奢。

重湖叠巘清嘉⑧,有三秋桂子⑨,十里荷花。羌管弄晴⑩,菱歌泛夜⑪,嬉嬉钓叟莲娃⑫。千骑拥高牙⑬,乘醉听箫鼓,吟赏烟霞。异日图将好景,归去凤池夸⑭。

⑬高牙:高大的牙旗。牙旗本指古代军前大旗或将帅大旗,此指达官贵人。

⑭凤池:凤凰池,指朝廷最高行政机关中书省。

A place of scenic beauty in the southeast
The metropolis in the region of the Three Wu's,
Qiantang has flourished since ancient times.
Clouded willow trees and bright painted bridges,
Windbreak window drapes and kingfisher-feathered curtains,
A hundred thousand houses clustered high and low.
Towering trees line the sandy bank,
The raging tide rolls upward like frost and snow,
The heavenly moat stretches to the horizon.
The market filled with tiers of pearls and gems;
Households overflowing with silks and satins,
Contend in wealth and luxury.

The clear twin lakes[①] and green hills offer picturesque views;
The fragrance of sweet osmanthus lingers on the autumn air,
Lotus flowers bloom far and wide in summer.
The sound of flutes soars up to the sunny skies,
The singing of folk songs breaks the silence of night,
Happy are the old anglers and girls collecting water chestnuts.
With a flag surrounded by a mounted retinue a thousand strong,
To enjoy music while in my cups,
To chant verses while admiring the mist and clouds at twilight.
When, one day, you win promotion with glory,
You will praise this place at Phoenix Pool profusely. [②]

---

① The West Lake which is divided by hills into the inner lake and the outer
lake.

② The imperial cabinet, or the court in general.

柳永词擅写游子之情，本词正是这方面的代表作。上片写悲秋，下片抒羁旅离别之苦。其中，"渐霜风凄紧，关河冷落，残照当楼"三句，颇受后人称道。

对潇潇暮雨洒江天①，一番洗清秋。渐霜风凄紧②，关河冷落③，残照当楼④。是处红衰翠减⑤，苒苒物华休⑥。惟有长江水，无语东流。

不忍登高临远⑦，望故乡渺邈⑧，归思难收⑨。叹年来踪迹，何事苦淹留⑩？想佳人、妆楼凝望⑪，误几回、天际识归舟⑫？争知我、倚阑干处⑬，正恁凝愁⑭。

①潇潇：小雨的样子。

②霜风：秋风。 凄紧：凄清而急剧。

③关河：泛指山河。关，关塞。

④残照：落日。

⑤是处：到处。红衰翠减：花木凋零。

⑥苒苒：即"冉冉"，渐渐。物华：美好的景物。

⑦临远：望远。

⑧渺邈(miǎo 秒)：遥远的样子。

⑨归思：想回故乡的情绪。

⑩何事：为什么。 淹留：久留。

⑪"误几回"句：多次错把远方驶来的船，当作爱人归来的船。

⑫争：怎。

⑬恁(rèn 任)：如此。

⑭凝愁：深愁。

I face the pattering rain in the evening sky over the river.
It refreshes the cool autumn at one sweep.
Gradually the frosty wind grows colder and stronger,
The landscape is cheerless and desolate,
The sunset lights up the pavilion.
All the red flowers and green leaves have faded.
Gradually the regaling views of nature die out.
Only the waters of the Yangtze River
Silently flow to the east.

I cannot bear to climb high and look far,
For when I gaze towards my hometown, too distant to see,
It is hard to suppress my longing.
Bemoaning my wanderings in recent years,
Why am I stubborn and stay away so long?
I see my beloved staring into the distance vainly seeking
A homeward boat that carries me to her.
How can she know that I am
Leaning against the parapet engrossed in such sorrowful thoughts?

王国维以此词引发妙喻,认为"古今之成大事业、大学问者,罔不经过三种之境界:'昨夜西风凋碧树,独上高楼,望尽天涯路。'此第一境界也。'衣带渐宽终不悔,为伊消得人憔悴。'此第二境界也。'众里寻他千百度,蓦然回首,那人却在、灯火阑珊处。'此第三境界也。"

槛菊愁烟兰泣露①,罗幕轻寒②,燕子双飞去。明月不谙离恨苦③,斜光到晓穿朱户④。

昨夜西风凋碧树⑤,独上高楼,望尽天涯路。欲寄彩笺兼尺素⑥,山长水阔知何处!

①槛(jiàn见):栏杆。兰泣露:兰草沾着露水,象在哭泣。

②罗幕:丝织的帷帘。

③谙(ān安):熟悉,懂得。

④朱户:红色的门。

⑤凋碧树:使树上的绿叶枯败凋落。

⑥彩笺(jiān兼):供题诗和写信用的精美纸张。此指怀念、相思的诗。尺素:指书信。

The chrysanthemum is vexed by the mist;
The orchid weeps in the dew.
Behind the gauze curtain, the air is cool.
A pair of swallows flies away.
Knowing not the bitter taste of separation,
The slanting moonlight lingers till dawn at the vermilion door.

Last night the west wind withered the green trees.
Alone I climbed the high pavilion,
Gazing at the distant road vanishing into the horizon.
I long to send you a letter but I have no coloured paper.
Oh where, past the endless mountains and rivers, are you?

欧阳修的词清丽明快,近似晏殊,均沿袭晚唐五代的婉约词风。本诗佳处在于构思之巧,上片渲染游子一触即发、渐行渐深的离愁,下片翻转笔墨,以空灵的笔触设想思妇的愁苦。一唱三叹,别具匠心。

候馆梅残①,溪桥柳细,草熏风暖摇征辔②。离愁渐远渐无穷,迢迢不断如春水③。

寸寸柔肠④,盈盈粉泪⑤,楼高莫近危栏倚⑥。平芜尽处是春山⑦,行人更在春山外。

①候馆:迎候宾客的馆舍。这里泛指旅舍。

②熏:原指香草,这里引申为香气。摇征辔(pèi 佩):指骑马远行。辔,驾驭牲口用的嚼子和缰绳。

③迢迢:原指路途遥远,这里有绵长的意思。

④寸寸柔肠:指非常伤心,有如肝肠寸断。

⑤盈盈:这里指泪水充溢的样子。粉泪:指女子的眼泪。

⑥危栏:高楼上的栏杆。

⑦平芜:平原上的草地。

Faded plum blossoms by the lonely posthouse,
Slender willow twigs by the bridge over the brook.
Through scented grass, in the warm breeze, rocked on horseback,
Far he wanders, his grief great at parting,
Like a long river in springtime, flowing endlessly.

She is broken-hearted,
With tears on her powdered cheeks.
Let her not lean over the balcony of the high tower.
Beyond the wilderness lie the spring hills,
And beyond them is the traveller.

河北民·王安石(1021—1086)

本诗是王安石早期诗作中的代表作。描写百姓荒年逃亡、丰年缺衣少吃的惨状,反映北宋积弱不振、虐政害民的社会现实,体现了诗人改革朝政的愿望。继承白居易新乐府的传统,主题明确突出,有强烈的针砭时弊的社会功用。

河北民①,生长二边长苦辛②。
家家养子学耕织,输与官家事夷狄③。
今年大旱千里赤,州县仍催给河役④。
老小相依来就南⑤,南人丰年自无食⑥。
悲愁天地白日昏,路旁过者无颜色⑦。
汝生不及贞观中⑧,斗粟数钱无兵戎⑨!

①河北:指黄河以北、白沟河以南地区,宋时于此设河北路。

②二边:指宋同辽与西夏的边境。宋、辽于河北以白沟河为界。

③事夷狄:宋每年以银十万两、绢二十万匹给辽;银五万两、绢十三万四、茶二万斤给西夏,称为岁币,作为求得边界安宁的代价。

④河役:治理黄河的劳役。

⑤就南:指秋收时到黄河以南逐熟求食。

⑥丰年自无食:赋税重,积欠多,丰年时官债私债逼得更紧。

⑦无颜色:形容愁容惨淡,面色苍白。

⑧贞观:唐太宗年号(627—649)。

⑨斗粟数钱:据说唐贞观时连年丰收,每斗米价仅三、四文钱。无兵戎:唐贞观时四边无战事。

224

Hard the lot of the people who live north of the river
On the borders of the Khitans and the Tanguts;
Each household brings up its children to farm and weave
But officials present the fruits to the barbarians.
In this year of great drought a thousand *li* lie waste,
Yet the magistrates press conscripts to work on the river;
Leading their old and young by the hand they flee south
Where the harvest was good — but the people there too have no
    food.
Grief afflicts heaven and earth, makes dark the day,
Even passersby turn pale.
If only you could have lived in the reign of Zhenguan[1]
When grain cost but a few cash a peck and there was no war!

---

[1]   This Tang emperor's reign (AD 627-649) was remembered as a period of
peace and prosperity.

全诗借写内部庭院、外围环境，称誉庭院主人湖阴先生。前两句以朴素平实之笔写庭院之整洁清幽，见出湖阴先生的洁志雅好。后两句描写庭院的外部环境，将青山、绿水人格化，衬托出湖阴先生与诗人的隐逸情怀。

"湖阴先生"为杨德逢的别号，曾与王安石为邻。此诗是题在杨德逢家墙壁上的。

茅檐长扫净无苔①，
花木成畦手自栽②。
一水护田将绿绕，
两山排闼送青来③。

①长扫：常扫。
②成畦(qí 奇)：田园中分划的小区。
③排闼(tà 踏)：推门而入。闼，小门。

His well-swept path under thatched eaves is clear of moss,
The flowers and trees here are planted by his hand;
A stream like an emerald girdle guards his fields
And the two hills confronting his gate cast a green shade.

晏几道是晏殊之子,词作造诣高于其父。题材虽不过爱情相思,但措辞婉妙,语浅情真,有浓重的个人身世之感。本词中"落花人独立,微雨燕双飞",虽为借用五代翁宏《春残》之诗句,但融情入景,与寂寞凄清的氛围构成有机的整体,赋予了诗句更深厚的内涵。

梦后楼台高锁,酒醒帘幕低垂①。去年春恨却来时②,落花人独立,微雨燕双飞③。

记得小蘋初见④,两重心字罗衣⑤,琵琶弦上说相思。当时明月在,曾照彩云归⑥。

①"梦后"两句:意谓人去楼空,欢情早已成为过去,反映出作者的凄寂心境。

②春恨:指由春日离别而引起的感伤情绪。却:再。

③"落花"两句:引用翁宏《春残》中诗句:"又是春残也,如何出翠帏?落花人独立,微雨燕双飞。"

④小蘋:当时一个歌女的名字。

⑤心字罗衣:有"心"字形花纹的丝织衣裳。

⑥彩云:比喻美女。这里指小蘋。

228

Awaking from a dream in the locked pavilion,
I sober up to see the curtain hanging low.
Last spring's grief again assails me.
Amidst the falling flowers she stood alone;
While in the light drizzle, pairs of swallows played.

I recall my first encounter with Xiao Pin; ①
She wore a light silk dress, embroidered with two hearts.
The music of her lute expressed her tender feelings.
Though the bright moon still shines,
The same moon sent away the rosy cloud.

① This was the name of a singsong girl.

水调歌头(明月几时有)·苏轼(1037—1101)

这首词是中秋词中最著名的一首,也是苏轼脍炙人口的旷达词。由中秋月色产生联想,融入有关月亮的神话传说和前人诗句,结合自己的失意情绪,道出出世与入世的矛盾心理。以浪漫洒脱的个性,创造出空灵飘逸的意境,阐明深刻的人生哲理。

丙辰中秋①,欢饮达旦,大醉,作此篇兼怀子由②。

明月几时有?把酒问青天③。不知天上宫阙④,今夕是何年?我欲乘风归去,又恐琼楼玉宇⑤,高处不胜寒。起舞弄清影,何似在人间。

转朱阁⑥,低绮户⑦,照无眠。不应有恨⑧,何事长向别时圆⑨?人有悲欢离合,月有阴晴圆缺,此事古难全。但愿人长久,千里共婵娟⑩。

①丙辰:宋神宗熙宁九年(1076)。

②子由:苏轼之弟苏辙的字,当时苏辙在济南。

③把酒:端起酒杯。

④宫阙:指月宫。

⑤琼楼玉宇:玉石砌的楼宇,指月中宫殿。

⑥转朱阁:是说月光从朱红色的华美楼阁的一面转到另一面。

⑦低绮户:月光低低地照进华美的窗户。

⑧"不应"句:月亮不应该有什么遗憾事吧?恨:憾,不满意。

⑨"何事"句:月亮为什么总是在人们不能团聚的时候圆呢?

⑩婵娟:指嫦娥,实指明月。

On the Mid-Autumn Festival of the year Bingchen[①] I drank *happily till dawn and wrote this in my cups while thinking of Ziyou*.[②]

Bright moon, when was your birth?
Winecup in hand, I ask the deep blue sky;
Not knowing what year it is tonight
In those celestial palaces on high.
I long to fly back on the wind,
Yet dread those crystal towers, those courts of jade,
Freezing to death among those icy heights!
Instead I rise to dance with my pale shadow;
Better off, after all, in the world of men.

Rounding the red pavilion,
Stooping to look through gauze windows,
She shines on the sleepless.
The moon should know no sadness;
Why, then, is she always full when dear ones are parted?
For men the grief of parting, joy of reunion,
Just as the moon wanes and waxes, is bright or dim:
Always some flaw — and so it has been since of old.
My one wish for you, then, is long life
And a share in this loveliness far, far away!

---

①   The year 1076.
②   His brother.

念奴娇·赤壁怀古·苏轼(1037—1101)

苏轼在词史上的一大贡献是"以诗为词",打破了"诗庄词媚"的传统界限,以词来表现诗的题材,"无意不可入,无事不可言",扩大了词的境界。本词属咏史怀古之作,歌颂江山之胜,仰怀古人,抒发作者的胸襟抱负和怀才不遇的感慨。

"赤壁"此指黄州(今湖北黄冈)赤壁矶,亦称赤鼻矶。

大江东去①,浪淘尽、千古风流人物。故垒西边②,人道是、三国周郎赤壁。乱石穿空③,惊涛拍岸④,卷起千堆雪⑤。江山如画,一时多少豪杰。

遥想公瑾当年⑥,小乔初嫁了,雄姿英发。羽扇纶巾⑦,谈笑间、樯橹灰飞烟灭⑧。故国神游⑨,多情应笑我,早生华发。人生如梦,一樽还酹江月⑩。

①大江:长江。

②故垒:旧时的军事营垒。

③乱石穿空:石壁直插高空。

④惊涛:巨浪。

⑤千堆雪:指无数的浪花。

⑥小乔:乔玄有二女,皆国色。大乔嫁孙策,小乔嫁周瑜。

⑦羽扇:羽毛做成的扇子。纶(guān 关)巾:青丝带做的头巾。

⑧樯橹:代指曹操的军队。樯,船上的桅杆。橹,桨的一种。

⑨故国:此指赤壁,古战场。神游:指对赤壁破曹故事的遐想。

⑩樽:酒杯。酹(lèi 类):倒酒祭奠。

232

East flows the mighty river,
Sweeping away the heroes of times past;
This ancient rampart on its western shore
Is Zhou Yu's Red Cliff of Three Kingdoms' fame;
Here jagged boulders pound the clouds,
Huge waves tear banks apart,
And foam piles up a thousand drifts of snow;
A scene fair as a painting,
Countless the brave men here in time gone by!

I dream of Marshal Zhou Yu in his day
With his new bride, the Lord Qiao's younger daughter,
Dashing and debonair,
Silk-capped, with feather fan,
He laughed and jested
While the dread enemy fleet was burned to ashes!
In fancy through those scenes of old I range,
My heart overflowing, surely a figure of fun.
A man grey before his time.
Ah, this life is a dream,
Let me drink to the moon on the river!

这是苏轼最早的一首豪放词。晚唐五代以来,词始终以婉约为主要风格。苏轼则一洗绮罗香泽之态,开创了豪放刚健的词风,打破了婉约词一统词坛的局面,为南宋形成婉约、豪放词的共同繁荣奠定了基础。

"密州"位于今山东省诸城县。

老夫聊发少年狂①,左牵黄②,右擎苍③,锦帽貂裘④,千骑卷平冈⑤。为报倾城随太守⑥,亲射虎,看孙郎⑦。

酒酣胸胆尚开张⑧,鬓微霜,又何妨!持节云中,何日遣冯唐⑨?会挽雕弓如满月⑩,西北望,射天狼⑪。

①狂:放荡无拘束,此指豪情壮怀。

②左牵黄:左手牵着黄狗。

③右擎(qíng 晴)苍:右臂架着苍鹰。

④锦帽:锦缎帽子。貂(diāo 刁)裘(qiú 求):貂鼠皮袍。

⑤千骑(jì 计):言随从之多,虚数。卷平冈:席卷平坦的山冈。

⑥"为报"句:为了报答全城百姓随太守出猎的盛意。倾,尽。

⑦孙郎:指三国时孙权。一次孙权骑马,马为猛虎所伤,权以双戟投掷,猛虎为之倒退。这里作者以孙权自比。

⑧"酒酣"句:痛饮兴浓,胸怀开阔,胆气豪壮。

⑨"持节"二句:《史记·张释之冯唐列传》载,汉文帝时,魏尚为云中郡太守,匈奴不敢进犯,后因报功状上多报了六颗首级,被削职判刑。冯唐指出文帝赏罚不当,文帝采纳了冯唐的意见,派遣冯唐持节赦魏尚,复以魏尚为云中守。节,使者所持的用竹竿做成的符信。云中,汉郡名,在今内蒙古自治区托克托县一带。诗人以魏尚自比,是说,什么时候派人来赦免我的过错,使我得到重用呢?

⑩会:将要,有预期的意思。雕弓:弓背上刻有花纹的弓。

⑪天狼:星名,主侵掠,这里代指辽和西夏。

Old limbs regain the fire of youth:
Left hand leashing a hound,
On the right wrist a falcon.
Silk-capped and sable-coated,
A thousand horsemen sweep across the plain;
The whole city, it's said, has turned out
To watch His Excellency
Shoot the tiger!

Heart gladdened by wine,
Who cares
For a few white hairs?
But when will the court send an envoy
With an imperial tally to pardon the exile?
That day I will bend my bow like a full moon
And aiming northwest
Shoot down the Wolf① from the sky!

---

① Sirius, symbolizing here the Qiang tribesmen then fighting with the Hans.

苏轼的题画诗。题画诗盖始于杜甫，如《画鹰》便是一例，杜甫之后，继之者不多。直至宋代，始渐盛行。本诗继承了杜甫以来题画诗的优秀传统，不局限于书画境，而是根据诗人自身的观察体会，拓展诗情，阐发人生哲理。

"惠崇"为宋初的诗僧和画家。

竹外桃花三两枝，
春江水暖鸭先知。
蒌蒿满地芦芽短①，
正是河豚欲上时②。

①蒌(lóu 楼)蒿：草名。

②河豚(tún 屯)：鱼名，味美而有毒。上：溯江而上。

Two or three sprays of peach behind bamboo;
When spring warms the river the ducks are the first to know;
Mayweed covers the ground, the reeds begin to shoot;
This is the season when porpoises swim upstream.

秦观与苏轼交往甚密，是传说中苏小妹三难新郎中的新郎。由于仕途坎坷，加上为人多愁善感，因而词风凄婉，与晏几道被并称为"古之伤心人"。本词是秦观一首著名的感伤词，"自在飞花轻似梦，无边丝雨细如愁"一句最为动人。

漠漠轻寒上小楼①，晓阴无赖似穷秋②，淡烟流水画屏幽③。

自在飞花轻似梦④，无边丝雨细如愁，宝帘闲挂小银钩⑤。

①漠漠：云烟密布的样子。轻寒：微寒。

②晓阴：春阴的早晨。无赖：无奈，无可奈何。穷秋：深秋。

③淡烟流水：是屏上所绘的风景。幽：暗。

④自在飞花：是说飞花飘忽不定，含有飞花无情无义的意思。

⑤"宝帘"句：是说把宝帘闲挂在小银钩上。宝帘，华美的帘子。闲挂，闲放不卷的意思。

Ascending the small pavilion in the light chill mist,
Clouds at daybreak, like a weary autumn day;
A pale haze and dark winding stream painted on screens.

Falling petals, leisurely, carefree, as in a dream;
The endless rain, sad as my grief at parting;
While pearl curtains hang idle on silver hooks.

苏幕遮(燎沉香)·周邦彦(1057—1121)

周邦彦是北宋集婉约派之大成的词人。本词不过是抒发在外作客的思乡之情,但"燎"、"消"、"呼"、"窥"字字生动传神,尤其"叶上初阳"三句,精妙地刻画出日照之荷、雨润之荷、风动之荷的神韵,体现出周词的士大夫风格,成为众口传诵的写荷名句。

燎沉香①,消溽暑②。鸟雀呼晴,侵晓窥檐语③。叶上初阳干宿雨④,水面清圆,一一风荷举。

故乡遥,何日去?家住吴门⑤,久作长安旅⑥。五月渔郎相忆否?小楫轻舟,梦入芙蓉浦⑦。

①燎:烧。沉香:又名水沉香,用沉香木做的香料。

②溽(rù入)暑:盛夏湿热的天气。

③侵晓:天刚亮。

④宿雨:昨夜下的雨。

⑤吴门:苏州别称,此借指周邦彦家乡钱塘。

⑥长安:这里借指宋都汴京。旅:客。

⑦芙蓉浦:开着荷花的浅水湖的汊口。

240

Burning eaglewood incense,
To avert the sultry summer heat;
Birds hailing the fine day
Peep out, chirping under eaves at daybreak.
The morning sun dries the overnight rain,
Now fresh and round over the water,
As below swaying lotus leaves rise and fall on the breeze.

My hometown is far away,
When can I go back?
My home is in Wumen, ①
But long I've stayed in the capital. ②
The May anglers may miss me or not,
But, in a light boat with small oars,
In my dreams I sail back to their Lotus Flower Pond.

---

① Present-day Suzhou, Jiangsu Province.
② Present-day Kaifeng, Henan Province.

周邦彦词浑厚典雅,讲究辞藻。本篇亦是其风格的完美体现。体物言情,穷极工巧,而文辞藻绘,音声和畅,自是一派闲雅气度,但若论情深意远,不免落于人后,同是抒写离情,柳三变《雨霖铃》就更是动人心魄。

水浴清蟾①,叶喧凉吹②,巷陌马声初断。闲依露井③,笑扑流萤,惹破画罗轻扇④。人静夜久凭阑⑤,愁不归眠,立残更箭⑥。叹年华一瞬,人今千里,梦沉书远⑦。

空见说,鬓怯琼梳⑧,容消金镜⑨,渐懒趁时匀染⑩。梅风地溽,虹雨苔滋⑪,一架舞红都变⑫。谁信无聊为伊⑬,才减江淹⑭,情伤荀倩⑮。但明河影下⑯,还看稀星数点。

①清蟾:指月亮。

②凉吹:指凉风。

③露井:指没有井亭遮覆的水井。

④"笑扑"两句:化用杜牧《秋夕》诗"银烛秋光冷画屏,轻罗小扇扑流萤"句。

⑤阑:栏杆。

⑥更(gēng 耕)箭:古代用铜壶滴漏计时,壶中立箭(相当于现在的指针)以指示刻度,标明时间。又称漏箭。

⑦书:这里指书信。

⑧琼梳:华贵的梳子。

⑨金镜:铜镜。

⑩匀染:指梳妆打扮。

⑪虹雨:指雷雨,夏天雨后往往有虹出现,故云。苔滋:青苔滋蔓,越长越多。

⑫舞红:飞红,即落花。

⑬伊:这里指作者所思念的女子。

⑭才减江淹:指作者因为过于思念他所追忆的那位女子,以致才情减退。

⑮情伤荀倩:指作者因为过于思念他所追忆的那位女子,以致神情恍惚起来。

⑯明河:指银河,即天河。

The moon was clear and bright after a bath,
Leaves rustled in the cool wind,
Hoofbeats faded in the lanes and streets.
Leisurely I leant against the well railing,
Watching her swatting merrily at fireflies,
Till eventually her silk gauze fan became torn.
Alas, a year has elapsed in a flash!
In the quiet night, long I've leant on the rail,
So depressed that I cannot sleep,
Lingering in the nostalgia of small hours.
We are severed so far apart now,
I no longer conjure her in my dreams nor do I receive her word.

I seem to see, her hair shaggy and unkempt,
Her face haggard in a bronze mirror,
She's grown too slothful to apply rouge and powder;
The ground is damp in the wet monsoon,
And after rainfall moss grows everywhere,
A bleak scene with red petals blown adrift.
Who knows that I'm brought so low over her,
Like the scholar whose literary grace is exhausted,
Like the man deeply mourning his dead wife?
All I can do is to gaze at the stars sparse above
Twinkling faintly beside the dull Milky Way.

渔家傲(天接云涛连晓雾)·李清照(1084—1155?)

李清照词多含蓄委婉,而本词却以广阔的胸襟、豪放的个性描述词人对理想的精神世界的执著追求。难怪梁启超曾说:"此绝似苏、辛派,不类《漱玉词》中语。"

天接云涛连晓雾①,星河欲转千帆舞②。仿佛梦魂归帝所③,闻天语④,殷勤问我归何处。

我报路长嗟日暮⑤,学诗谩有惊人句⑥。九万里风鹏正举⑦,风休住,蓬舟吹取三山去⑧。

①云涛:云如波涛起伏。

②星河:银河。

③帝所:天帝的住所。

④闻天语:听见天帝说话。

⑤报:回答。嗟:嗟叹。

⑥谩有:徒有,空有。谩,通"漫"。

⑦举:鸟飞翔的意思。这里借以自喻。

⑧蓬舟:像蓬草一样轻快的小舟。三山:即蓬莱、方丈、瀛洲三座山。

In the sky merged with the floating clouds and morning mist,
The Milky Way is about to fade, a thousand sails dancing;
It seems in a dream that I've returned to the Heavenly Palace,
And heard the Jade Emperor speaking,
Eagerly asking where I am bound.

I reply that life's road is long and I'm ageing,
What I've achieved is a few unusual poems.
Now the mighty roc of nine thousand *li* has taken wing.
May the wind keep blowing
My little boat to the land of the immortals.

如梦令(昨夜雨疏风骤)·李清照(1084—1155?)

李清照是婉约词派的代表作家。本篇当是易安前期作品,"雨疏风骤"、"绿肥红瘦"状物极是自然清新、传神有致,虽花容憔悴,亦只觉时序代换,从容可喜。易以他时,当只知"红瘦"而不觉"绿肥"矣,境由心生,斯言诚哉。

昨夜雨疏风骤①,浓睡不消残酒②。试问卷帘人③,却道"海棠依旧"。"知否?知否?应是绿肥红瘦④。"

①疏:稀。骤:急。

②浓睡:酣睡。残酒:残留的醉意。

③卷帘人:指侍女。

④绿肥红瘦:叶茂花稀。

Last night the rain was light, the wind fierce,
And deep sleep did not dispel the effects of wine.
When I ask the maid rolling up the curtains,
She answers, "The crab-apple blossoms look the same."
I cry, "Can't you see? Can't you see?
The green leaves are fresh but the red flowers are fading!"

这是李清照晚年所作的一首元夕词，以元宵佳节的热闹景象，反衬词人历尽沧桑、国破家亡的凄苦心境。强烈的盛衰之感，令人闻之泣下。辛弃疾、刘辰翁等都曾仿其调而和之。

落日熔金①，暮云合璧②，人在何处③？染柳烟浓④，吹梅笛怨⑤，春意知几许？元宵佳节，融和天气，次第岂无风雨⑥？来相召，香车宝马⑦，谢他酒朋诗侣⑧。

中州盛日⑨，闺门多暇，记得偏重三五⑩。铺翠冠儿⑪，捻金雪柳⑫，簇带争济楚⑬。如今憔悴，风鬟雾鬓⑭，怕见夜间出去⑮。不如向帘儿底下，听人笑语。

①落日熔金：夕阳如正在熔化的黄金那样灿烂。

②暮云合璧：暮云连成一片，就象璧玉合成一块一样。

③人：这里是作者自指。

④染柳烟浓：指柳树笼罩在浓浓的雾霭里。

⑤吹梅笛怨：笛子吹出《梅花落》曲幽怨的声音。

⑥次第：接着，转眼。

⑦香车宝马：指装饰华美的车马。

⑧"谢他"句：指谢绝"酒朋诗侣"的邀请。

⑨中州：在今河南省，古时称中州或豫州。这里指北宋都城汴京(今河南省开封市)。盛日：指汴京沦陷以前的繁荣兴盛时期。

⑩三五：旧历每月十五。这里特指正月十五，即元宵节。

⑪铺翠冠儿：饰有翠鸟羽毛的女式帽子。

⑫捻金雪柳：用金线搓丝扎制成的雪柳。雪柳，宋代元宵节妇女头上戴的一种装饰物。

⑬簇带：宋时俗语，插戴的意思。济楚：整齐、端丽。

⑭风鬟雾鬓：头发蓬松散乱。

⑮怕见：懒得。

The setting sun like melted gold,
Evening clouds like jade,
But where has my love gone?
Dense mist hangs over the newly sprouted willow,
The melancholy tune of a flute lingers amidst plum blossoms.
But who knows this is but a glimpse of spring?
At the Lantern Festival,
The weather is fine,
But who knows if there will not be a sudden storm?
A fragrant carriage with rare stallions has been sent to fetch me,
Yet I decline the invitation of my friends for wine and poetry.

In our country's prosperous days, in the capital,
I had plenty of leisure time as a girl;
I still remember my liking for the Lantern Festival.
My head adorned with jade,
Wearing ornaments of gold,
My new clothes were gorgeous.
But now I'm pale and sallow,
My hair ruffled by the wind, tinged grey by the mist,
I fear to go out at night.
Better to hide behind the bamboo curtain
Listening to the laughter of others.

本诗显示了陆游创作七律的高超技巧。首联渲染丰收之年农村的宁静、欢愉气象；次联写山水景色，寓含哲理；第三联描摹赞颂古朴的民风民俗；末联笔锋一转，抒发了诗人安于农村平静生活的志趣。

"山西村"位于今浙江省山阴县。

莫笑农家腊酒浑，丰年留客足鸡豚①。
山重水复疑无路，柳暗花明又一村。
箫鼓追随春社近，衣冠简朴古风存②。
从今若许闲乘月，拄杖无时夜叩门③。

①腊酒：头年腊月（农历十二月）酿的酒。豚(tún 屯)：小猪。

②春社：古代以立春后第五个戊日为春社日，这一天祭土地神祈丰年。

③乘月：趁月，趁着月夜出游。无时：随时。

Don't sneer at the lees in the peasants' wine,
In a good year they've chicken and pork to offer guests.
Where hills bend, streams wind and the pathway seems to end,
Past dark willows and flowers in bloom lies another village.
They greet the spring sacrifice here with pipes and drums,
And dress simply, keeping up the old traditions.
Some evening when I'm free and there is moonlight,
I shall stroll over with my stick and knock at their gate.

本诗以"和戎诏下"为核心,从不同角度选取最有感染力的典型事例,形成鲜明对比。以凝练简洁的语言,从"十五年"的时间范围抚事伤时,深刻地鞭挞了南宋朝廷的卖国苟安,反映了戍边将士报国无路的景状和中原遗民渴望恢复中原的强烈愿望。

和戎诏下十五年,将军不战空临边①。
朱门沉沉按歌舞,厩马肥死弓断弦②。
戍楼刁斗催落月,三十从军今白发③。
笛里谁知壮士心?沙头空照征人骨④。
中原干戈古亦闻,岂有逆胡传子孙⑤!
遗民忍死望恢复,几处今宵垂泪痕⑥。

①"和戎"句:指隆兴元年(1163)的宋金和议,至淳熙四年(1177)首尾正好十五年。

②沉沉:深远貌。厩(jiù 救):马房。

③戍楼:边防的岗楼。刁斗:军中打更用的铜器。

④笛:《关山月》为汉示府横吹曲名,用笛吹奏。

⑤"岂有"句:这句是说历史上少数民族入侵进占中原,没有能传上几代的。

⑥遗民:指留在金统治区的北宋遗民。忍死:不死以待。

252

For fifteen years we have made peace with the Tartars,
Our frontier generals rest idle, their swords sheathed;
Deep within vermilion gates there is singing and dancing,
Horses die plump in their stables, bowstrings are broken,
And the tocsin simply hastens the waning moon,
While the hair of the men who joined up at thirty is white.
Who can gauge a soldier's heart from the sound of his flute?
Did they perish in vain, those whose bones gleam white on the
  sand?
Since ancient times war has raged on the Central Plain —
Will the sons of the Huns plague us still, and their sons' sons?
A subject people, weary to death, longs for freedom,
There is no counting the tears that flow tonight!

"处江湖之远,则忧
其君"。纵是沈居草莽,
亦无非家国之思。惟赤
心爱国如陆放翁,方能
作如此真挚之语,读放
翁诗,每觉有一腔忠愤
之气,直欲破纸而出。
希文若得见放翁,当不
致有"吾谁与归"之叹。

僵卧孤村不自哀,
尚思为国戍轮台①。
夜阑卧听风吹雨②,
铁马冰河入梦来。

①轮台:在今新疆维吾尔自治
区轮台县。汉唐时曾在这里屯兵。
②夜阑:夜将尽。

Stark I lie in a lonely village, uncomplaining,
And dream of defending Karashar for our state;
Late at night on my couch I hear the driving rain,
Iron-clad steeds cross a frozen river in my dreams.

《示儿》是陆游著名的爱国诗篇。为其临终前所写,既是绝笔,也是遗嘱。全诗毫无雕饰,直抒胸臆,一腔爱国之情、报国之志喷薄而出,悲壮沉痛,感人肺腑。

死去原知万事空,
但悲不见九州同①。
王师北定中原日,
家祭无忘告乃翁②!

①九州同:古代分中国为九州,九州同指祖国统一。

②乃翁:你的父亲,陆游自称。

Death ends all, that is sure,
But what grieves me is not to have seen our land united;
The day that our imperial arms win back the Central Plain,
Mind you sacrifice and let your old man know!

范成大晚年写《四时田园杂兴》共六十首,首次以大型组诗方式,生动真实地写出农家的忧喜悲欢和劳作生活,由此赢得了"田园诗人"的称号。本诗为"夏日"部分的第七首,以老农口吻,朴素简洁地正面描写农家的劳动场面,富有生活情趣和乡土气息。

昼出耘田夜绩麻①,
村庄儿女各当家。
童孙未解供耕织②,
也傍桑阴学种瓜③。

①耘(yún 云)田:除草。绩麻:把麻搓捻成线或绳。

②未解:不懂得,不会。供:担任,从事。

③傍(bàng 棒):靠近。

In the day farming and at night twisting hemp for rope,
Young men and women each help their families cope.
The grandchildren too small to plough and weave
Learn to plant a gourd under a mulberry tree.

范成大与杨万里、陆游、尤袤号称"中兴四大诗人"。诗作题材较丰富,既有田园诗,又有爱国诗等,尤其擅写民生民俗。本诗便是写织女们的劳动生活,不仅写到蚕茧的清香,还道出了劳作之艰辛和"抽尽新丝女颜老"的悲哀,令人耳目一新。

小麦青青大麦黄,原头日出天色凉①。
妇姑相呼有忙事,舍后煮茧门前香②。
缫车嘈嘈似风雨,茧厚丝长无断缕。
今年那暇织绢着,明日西门卖丝去③。

①"小麦"句取自汉童谣:"小麦青青大麦黄,谁其获者妇与姑。"

②妇姑:媳妇和婆婆。

③那(nó挪):作"哪"理解。着:穿。西门:指丝市聚集处。

When the barley is ripe the wheat is green still,
Upon the field the sun rises dispersing a chill.

The dames urge daughters-in-law in the back room
To boil the cocoons that release their perfume.

Silk wheels spin, a shower awoken;
Long threads spun, not a fibre broken.

But they cannot yet weave a blouse for themselves to wear.
Tomorrow they'll sell the silk at the West Gate Fair①

---

① West Gate Fair may be a silk market in the town. The village women had to sell their silk to cover the land tax before they could weave a piece of cloth for themselves.

辛词擅长借物抒情、借史抒情。本词上片由登临北固楼远眺的风光，引发山河沦陷的愁怨和英雄无用武之地的愤慨；下片追思史事，怀古伤今，寄托忧愤之情。全词激昂慷慨，是辛弃疾豪放词的代表作。

"建康"位于今江苏省南京市。

楚天千里清秋①，水随天去秋无际。遥岑远目②，献愁供恨，玉簪螺髻③。落日楼头，断鸿声里④，江南游子⑤，把吴钩看了⑥，栏杆拍遍，无人会，登临意。

休说鲈鱼堪脍，尽西风，季鹰归未？求田问舍，怕应羞见，刘郎才气。可惜流年，忧愁风雨，树犹如此！倩何人唤取，红巾翠袖，揾英雄泪！

①楚天：楚国一带地区。这里泛指江南地区。清秋：凄凉冷落的秋天。

②遥岑(cén岑)：远山。远目：远望。

③玉簪螺髻：比喻山。这些山有的象美人头上的碧玉簪，有的象螺旋形的发髻。

④断鸿：失群的孤雁。

⑤江南游子：客居江南的人，作者自指。

⑥吴钩：古吴国所造弯形宝刀，这里指佩剑。

A southern sky and a clear sweep of autumn,
Water brims to the skyline, autumn knows no bounds,
While in the distant hills,
Jade clasps on a girl's coiled tresses,
Only conjure up grief and pain.
High in the pavilion I watch the setting sun,
Hear the cry of a lonely swan,
A wanderer in the south, gazing at my sword,
I beat time on the balustrade,
With none to know
What passes through my mind.

楚天千里清秋,水随天去秋无际。遥岑远目,献愁供恨,玉簪螺髻。落日楼头,断鸿声里,江南游子,把吴钩看了,栏杆拍遍,无人会,登临意。

休说鲈鱼堪脍,尽西风,季鹰归未①?求田问舍,怕应羞见,刘郎才气②。可惜流年,忧愁风雨,树犹如此③!倩何人唤取,红巾翠袖④,揾英雄泪⑤!

①鲈鱼堪脍:晋代吴郡人张翰,字季鹰,在洛阳作官,因秋风起,想起家乡的鲈鱼脍,便辞官归去。堪,可以,正好。脍(kuài 快),把鱼肉切细。这两句的意思是说:不要说鲈鱼味道鲜美,尽管秋风吹来,我怎能象季鹰那样弃职还乡呢?

②求田问舍:购买田地、房产。三国时,刘备曾批评许汜(fàn 泛),只知求田问舍,无救世之意。刘郎:刘备。

③树犹如此:晋代桓温领兵北征,见自己早年栽的柳树已长大,感叹说:"木犹如此,人何以堪(人怎能经得住不老呢)!"

④红巾翠袖:少女的装束,这里借指歌女。倩:请。

⑤揾(wèn 问):擦。

True, this is the season for perch,
But will the west wind
Blow the wanderer home?[1]
Those who grub for houses and land
Must blush to meet a noble-hearted man. [2]
Ah, the years slip past
Lamented by wind and rain,
And even the trees grow old!
Who will summon a green-sleeved maid
With red handkerchief
To wipe the hero's tears?

---

[1] An allusion to Zhang Han, a scholar of the Jin Dynasty (AD 265-420), who gave up his office to return home when he saw it was autumn and the time to eat perch in the Yangtze Valley.

[2] At the end of the Han Dynasty (206 BC-AD 220) Chen Deng ignored Xu Fan because the latter was only interested in looking for good properties to buy, regardless of the fate of the empire.

以词描述农村风物，起于苏轼，辛弃疾继承发展了这一传统，写了若干首农村词，风格清新朴素、恬淡自然。本词不但描绘出一幅农村夏夜图，而且展现了农村的丰收景象和人们的喜悦之情，给人美的享受。

"黄沙道"位于今江西省上饶县西。

明月别枝惊鹊①，清风半夜鸣蝉。稻花香里说丰年，听取蛙声一片。

七八个星天外，两三点雨山前②。旧时茅店社林边③，路转溪桥忽见④。

①"明月"句：乌鹊因月色明亮而受惊，飞离枝头。

②天外：天边。

③社林：土地庙附近的树林。

④忽见：即忽现。"见"通"现"。

The bright moon startles the crow on the slanting bough,
At midnight the breeze is cool, cicadas shrill;
The fragrance of the paddy foretells a good year
And frogs croak far and wide.

Seven or eight stars above the horizon,
Two or three drops of rain before the hill;
An old thatched inn borders the wood with the local shrine,
And where the road bends a small bridge is suddenly seen.

本词引用了孙权、刘裕、宋文帝、廉颇等典故,由于运用贴切自然,不仅没有"掉书袋"之气,反而借古喻今,感时伤事,更显悲壮沉雄。

"京口"位于今江苏省镇江市;"北固亭"在镇江市东北北固山上,又名北顾亭。

千古江山,英雄无觅、孙仲谋处①。舞榭歌台②,风流总被③、雨打风吹去。斜阳草树,寻常巷陌,人道寄奴曾住④。想当年,金戈铁马,气吞万里如虎⑤。

元嘉草草,封狼居胥,赢得仓皇北顾。四十三年,望中犹记、烽火扬州路。可堪回首,佛狸祠下,一片神鸦社鼓!凭谁问:廉颇老矣,尚能饭否?

①孙仲谋:三国时吴主孙权字仲谋,曾在京口建都。

②舞榭(xiè 谢)歌台:歌舞的台榭。榭,台上的屋子。

③风流:指英雄业绩的余韵。

④寄奴:南朝宋武帝刘裕的小名,刘裕生长于京口。

⑤"金戈"二句:指刘裕两次率晋军北伐,灭南燕、后秦之事。

In this ancient land
What trace remains of Wu's brave king Sun Quan?①
Towers and pavilions where girls danced and sang,
Your glory is swept away by wind and rain;
The slanting sunlight falls on grass and trees,
Small lanes, the quarters of the humble folk;
Yet here, they say, Liu Yu② lived.
I think of the days gone by
When with gilded spear and iron-clad steed he charged
Like a tiger to swallow up vast territories.

---

①   A third-century king who reigned in Jingkou.
②   The first ruler of the Southern Song Dynasty in the fifth century and a native of this city, who led successful expeditions against the northern Tartars.

269

千古江山,英雄无觅、孙仲谋处。舞榭歌台,风流总被、雨打风吹去。斜阳草树,寻常巷陌,人道寄奴曾住。想当年,金戈铁马,气吞万里如虎。

元嘉草草,封狼居胥,赢得仓皇北顾①。四十三年,望中犹记、烽火扬州路②。可堪回首③,佛狸祠下④,一片神鸦社鼓⑤!凭谁问:廉颇老矣,尚能饭否⑥?

①"元嘉"三句:指宋文帝未作充分准备就北伐,终为北魏战败的往事。元嘉,刘裕之子宋文帝刘义隆年号(424—453)。 草草,草率马虎。 封狼居胥,北伐立功的意思。狼居胥,山名,在今内蒙古自治区西北部。汉将霍去病曾追击匈奴至此。 封山,筑土为坛,祭山神以纪念胜利。 赢得,落得。仓皇北顾,看到北方追来的敌人而惊惶失色。

②"四十三年"三句:四十三年前(1162年),辛弃疾投归南宋,途经扬州,曾眼见金兵在扬州一带烧杀的战火。

③可堪:哪堪,不堪。

④佛(bì 必)狸祠:故址在今江苏省六合县瓜步山上。元嘉二十六年(450),为北魏太武帝拓拔焘(小字佛狸)击败刘宋后所建。

⑤神鸦:吃庙里祭品的乌鸦。社鼓:社日祭神时的鼓声。

⑥"凭谁问"二句:廉颇为赵国名将,被人陷害,出奔魏国。后来,赵数困于秦,想起用廉颇,廉颇也想再为赵国效力。赵王派使者探看廉颇尚可用否。廉颇为之一饭斗米、肉十斤,披甲上马,以示可用。凭,靠。

In the days of Yuan Jia①
Hasty preparations were made
To march to the Langjuxu Mountains,②
But the men of Song were routed from the north.
Now forty-three years have passed,
And looking north I remember
The beacon fires that blazed the way to Yangzhou;③
Bitter memories these
Of sacred crows among the holy drums
In the Tartar emperor's temple,④
Who will ask old Lian Po⑤
If he still enjoys his food?

---

①   AD 424-453.

②   In Inner Mongolia, reached by the Han army after defeating the Huns in 119 BC.

③   In 1161 the Nüzhen Tartars occupied Yangzhou.

④   When Northern Wei, a Tartar Dynasty, defeated the Southern Song troops in the fifth century, their emperor built a temple near Yangzhou.

⑤   A brave general of the Warring States Period (475-221 BC), who to prove his ability to lead an army in his old age rode out in full armour after a hearty meal.

南乡子·登京口北固亭有怀·辛弃疾(1140—1207)

这是辛弃疾一首著名的登临怀古之作。词中融入了强烈的爱国之情,创造出雄奇深阔的意境,格调豪放激越。其词作内容无论深度、广度均超越前人。辛弃疾、苏轼在词史上同为豪放词派的杰出代表,并称"苏辛"。

何处望神州①? 满眼风光北固楼②。千古兴亡多少事,悠悠。不尽长江滚滚流。

年少万兜鍪③,坐断东南战未休④。天下英雄谁敌手? 曹刘⑤。生子当如孙仲谋⑥!

①神州:本指中国,这里指中原沦陷区。

②北固楼:即北固亭。

③年少:孙权继承孙策为吴主时,只有十九岁。万兜鍪(móu谋):指挥庞大军队的意思。兜鍪,古代打仗时戴的头盔。这里代指兵士。

④坐断:占据。

⑤曹刘:曹操、刘备。

⑥"生子"句:汉献帝建安十八年(213),曹操率军攻打濡须(今安徽省巢湖市),孙权迎战。曹操见其船只、军械、队伍非常严整,感叹说:"生子当如孙仲谋。刘景升(刘表)儿子若豚犬(猪狗)耳!"

Where can I see our northern territory?
Splendid the view from the Beigu Pavilion.
How many dynasties have risen and fallen
In the course of long centuries,
And history goes on
Endless as the swift-flowing Yangtze.

A young king[1] with a host of armoured men
Held the southeast and fought with never a moment's respite
Of all the empire's heroes two alone could match him —
Brave Cao Cao and Liu Bei.
"How I long for a son like Sun Quan!"[2]

---

[1]   Referring to Sun Quan who founded the Kingdom of Wu in the third century after the break-up of the Han empire. Wu occupied the lower reaches of the Yangtze; Shu, ruled by Liu Bei, was in the upper Yangtze Valley and Sichuan while north China was ruled by Cao Cao, whose son founded the Kingdom of Wei.

[2]   A remark made by Cao Cao.

扬州慢(淮左名都)·姜夔(1155?—1221?)

本词是姜夔的代表作。上片写扬州遭受金兵洗劫后的萧条景象。其中"犹厌言兵"一语,"包括无限伤乱语,他人累千百万,亦无此韵味"(清陈廷焯《白雪斋词话》)。下片借杜牧抒发"黍离"之感。词中运用反衬手法,如:昔日"名都",今成"空城";昔日"杜郎俊赏",今朝"难赋深情"等更加深了作者厌战、怀旧、关心国事的主题的揭示。

淳熙丙申至日①,予过维扬②。夜雪初霁,荠麦弥望③。入其城,则四顾萧条,寒水自碧,暮色渐起,戍角悲吟④。予怀怆然⑤,感慨今昔,因自度此曲⑥。千岩老人以为有《黍离》之悲也⑦。

淮左名都⑧,竹西佳处⑨,解鞍少驻初程⑩。过春风十里⑪,尽荠麦青青。自胡马窥江去后⑫,废池乔木,犹厌言兵。渐黄昏、清角吹寒,都在空城⑬。

杜郎俊赏,算而今、重到须惊。纵豆蔻词工,青楼梦好,难赋深情。二十四桥仍在,波心荡、冷月无声。念桥边红药,年年知为谁生?

① 淳熙丙申:淳熙三年(1176)。至日:冬至日。

②维扬:扬州。

③荠(jì 计)麦:荠菜和麦子。弥望:满眼。

④戍角:军营中的号角。

⑤ 予怀:我的心情。怆(chuàng 创)然:悲伤。

⑥自度此曲:自己创制了这个曲调。

⑦千岩老人:南宋诗人萧德藻,字东夫,号千岩老人。《黍离》之悲:象《诗经·王风·黍离》那样感伤国事艰危。

⑧淮左:宋置淮南东路和淮南西路。方位以东为左,所以东路简称淮左。扬州属淮南东路。名都:著名都会。

⑨竹西佳处:指扬州。竹西,亭名,在扬州城东禅智寺附近。

⑩少驻:小驻,短暂的停留。初程:旅途的第一阶段。

⑪春风十里:指扬州昔日繁华的街道。

⑫胡马窥江:指金兵进犯长江流域。胡马,指金兵。窥,偷伺。江,长江。

⑬"渐黄昏"二句:渐近黄昏时候,凄清的号角声在洗劫后的扬州城上空飘荡,更给人增加了凄凉之感。

On the winter solstice in the third year (1176) of the reign of
*Chunxi I passed by Yangzhou. When the snow let up, a stretch of field
cress met my eyes. I entered the city and looked around myself, only to
see a desolate scene and freezing blue waters. As dusk deepened, horns
could be heard from garrison barracks. Overwhelmed by grief, I com-
posed this tune. In Xiao Dezao's opinion, my poem is evocative of the
sadness expressed in the ancient lament "On a Fallen Capital."*

At the famous city east of Huaihe River
And west of a stretch of bamboo
(Where the first stage of my journey ends),
I dismount to rest.
As I walk along the road
Once bathed in a reach of vernal breezes
I see green field cress on all sides.
Since Tartar cavalry pressed upon the Yangtze,
The city with abandoned moat and towering trees
Still hates all mention of the war.
As evening sets in, in the empty city
Chilly horns are echoing.

淳熙丙申至日,予过维扬。夜雪初霁,荠麦弥望。入其城,则四顾萧条,寒水自碧,暮色渐起,戍角悲吟。予怀怆然,感慨今昔,因自度此曲。千岩老人以为有《黍离》之悲也。

淮左名都,竹西佳处,解鞍少驻初程。过春风十里,尽荠麦青青。自胡马窥江去后,废池乔木,犹厌言兵。渐黄昏、清角吹寒,都在空城。

杜郎俊赏①,算而今、重到须惊②。纵豆蔻词工③,青楼梦好④,难赋深情。二十四桥仍在⑤,波心荡、冷月无声。念桥边红药⑥,年年知为谁生?

①杜郎:指唐代诗人杜牧。俊赏:高明的鉴赏力。

②算:料想,估计之词。须:一定。

③豆蔻词:指杜牧的《赠别》诗:"娉娉袅袅十三余,豆蔻梢头二月初。"后称女子十三、四岁的年纪为豆蔻年华。豆蔻,植物名,形似芭蕉。工,工巧。

④青楼梦:杜牧《遣怀》诗:"落魄江南载酒行,楚腰纤细掌中轻。十年一觉扬州梦,赢得青楼薄幸名。"青楼,妓院。好:指"青楼梦"诗句之好,非指梦好。

⑤二十四桥:旧址在今扬州西郊,相传古有二十四个美人在此吹箫。

⑥红药:红芍药花。

If Du Mu① the connoisseur of bygone beauty
Returned to life, he'd lament the lost glory.
His magic pen that described a cardamon-like girl
And dream-like time in blue mansions
Can no more tell a romantic story.
The twenty-four bridges,
Upon which fairies once played their flutes,
Are still there;
And below, in ripples the silent moon glows.
But, oh, for whom the red peonies by the bridges
Bloom every spring? Who knows? Who knows?

---

① Du Mu (AD 803-852?), a poet of Yangzhou, famous for his poems about the city and the beautiful women there.

这一首咏梅词，上片着重咏梅之精神品格，下片着重咏梅之遭遇，抒爱花、惜花之意和抒花无力的感慨。比喻、象征手法的运用，是此词的显着特点，全篇一气用了五个典故，以历史、神话、传说和诗歌中的美人比拟梅花，将梅人格化；通篇不着一个梅字，而梅之精神全出，托喻之义，见于言外。

苔枝缀玉①，有翠禽小小，枝上同宿②。客里相逢③，篱角黄昏，无言自倚修竹④。昭君不惯胡沙远⑤，但暗忆、江南江北。想佩环、月夜归来，化作此花幽独⑥。

犹记深宫旧事，那人正睡里，飞近蛾绿。莫似春风，不管盈盈，早与安排金屋。还教一片随波去，又却怨、玉龙哀曲。等恁时、重觅幽香，已入小窗横幅。

①苔枝：长有苔藓的梅枝。缀玉：指梅花像玉一样缀在梅枝。

②翠禽：翠绿色的鸟。

③客里相逢：出门在外作客时与梅相遇。

④"无言"句：语出杜甫《佳人》诗："绝代有佳人，幽居在空谷。……天寒翠袖薄，日暮倚修竹。"修竹，高长的竹子。

⑤昭君：王嫱字昭君，西汉南郡秭归(今湖北省兴山县昭君村)人，元帝时宫女。匈奴呼韩邪单于入汉求和亲，昭君远嫁匈奴。胡沙：北方大沙漠。

⑥"想环佩"二句：语出杜甫《咏怀古迹》五首之三咏昭君诗：

"画图省(xǐng醒)识春风面，环佩空归月夜魂。"佩环，衣上所系的玉饰，此代昭君。幽独，幽怨孤独。

Upon a mossy bough dotted with jade
Tiny green birds perch in pairs.
It's evening far from my home
In a distant land at the corner of a hedge
Where a plum silently blooms against a bamboo grove.

It's said that once a beauty
Married to a northern chieftain
Was tormented by sandy winds.
She yearned for her home on the Yangtze.
So on a moonlit night her spirit
Flew back home with rings and pendants
And turned into a lonely plum.

苔枝缀玉，有翠禽小小，枝上同宿。客里相逢，篱角黄昏，无言自倚修竹。昭君不惯胡沙远，但暗忆、江南江北。想佩环、月夜归来，化作此花幽独。

犹记深宫旧事，那人正睡里，飞近蛾绿①。莫似春风，不管盈盈②，早与安排金屋③。还教一片随波去，又却怨、玉龙哀曲④。等恁时、重觅幽香⑤，已入小窗横幅⑥。

①"犹记"三句：用南朝宋武帝刘裕女寿阳公主事。"寿阳公主人日(阴历正月初七)卧于含章殿檐下，梅花落公主额上，成五出花，拂之不去。……宫女奇其异，竞效之，今梅花妆是也。"那人，指寿阳公主。蛾绿，指女子美丽的眉毛。

②盈盈：本用以形容美女，仪态美好的样子，此代指梅花。

③金屋：汉武帝幼时，姑母指着自己的女儿阿娇问他："好否？"他答："若得阿娇作妇，当以金屋贮之。"这句是把梅花比作美人，应当护持珍爱。

④玉龙哀曲：玉龙，笛子名。哀曲，指笛曲《梅花落》。

⑤恁(rèn 认)时：那时，指梅花落时。

⑥横幅：横挂的梅花画图。

Yet another story: once
The plum printed her petals
Upon the forehead of a sleeping princess
And all palace girls followed the style.

Oh, don't be as apathetic as the spring wind
Towards the beaming flowers!
You should cherish them, as you
Cherish a beauty in a golden nest. ①
When the petals are carried away by flowing water,
And you complain of the flute that trills "On Fallen Plum;"
Then you'll find their fragrant images
In the painted scroll by the window.

---

① Han-Dynasty Emperor Wudi (reigned 140-87 BC) said, "If I can have Ah
Jiao (his cousin and a beauty) as my wife, I'll put her in a golden house." Here the
poet compares plum flowers to a beauty.

本诗先描绘水乡景色，继而由写景转向景中之人。一幅优美的荡桨归家图，勾起诗人的乡愁。末句以一曲凄婉的《鹧鸪词》在反差中重新认识到嘉兴秀色，意气再度昂扬起来。

"嘉兴"位于今浙江省嘉兴县。

三山云海几千里，十幅蒲帆挂烟水①。
吴中过客莫思家，江南画船如屋里②。
芦芽短短穿碧沙，船头鲤鱼吹浪花③。
吴姬荡桨入城去，细雨小寒生绿纱④。
我歌《水调》无人续，江上月凉吹紫竹⑤。
春风一曲《鹧鸪》词，花落莺啼满城绿⑥。

①三山：旧时福州的别称。福州旧城中有九仙山（于山）、闽山、越王山三座山。十幅：指船帆的宽度。蒲帆：用蒲草做的船帆。烟水：雾霭苍茫的水面。

②吴中过客：经过吴中的旅客。这里是作者自谓。嘉兴为古吴国旧地。

③碧沙：碧水清浅见底，河沙看上去也象是碧色的。

④吴姬：吴地的女子。"细雨"句：是说细雨濛濛，略生寒意，水面泛起微波，如同皱起的绿纱。

⑤《水调》：商调曲调名。紫竹：指箫、笛一类竹管乐器。

⑥《鹧鸪》词：即《鹧鸪天》词，《鹧鸪天》是词牌名。词，别本作"吟"。

Thousands of miles, a sea of clouds, with three isles,
Ten sheets of rush sails carrying with them the water and mist;
The traveller in the land of Wu need not long for home,
For the painted Yangtze barge is like one's own room.
Tender rush shoots pierce through the green gauze curtain,
By the prow, carp are blowing bubbles in the waves.
As the local girl moves her oar to sail through the city,
It drizzles and feels cool amid the green rushes.
I sing a song but no one hears my singing,
The moon grows chill and the wind blows through the bamboos.
As the "Song of the Cuckoo" is sung in the spring breeze,
Blossoms fall, the oriole cries, and the whole city turns green.

这是一首登临怀古之作,该词是继王安石《金陵怀古》后最著名的金陵怀古词之一。写六朝古都金陵的衰落凄凉,抒发吊古伤今的情怀。感情深沉,气象开阔。"王谢堂前双燕子"一句引用刘禹锡《乌衣巷》诗句,并赋予新的意境,颇为后人传诵。

六代繁华春去也①,更无消息。空怅望,山川形胜,已非畴昔。王谢堂前双燕子②,乌衣巷口曾相识③。听夜深,寂寞打孤城,春潮急。

思往事,愁为织,怀故国,空陈迹。但荒烟衰草,乱鸦斜日,玉树歌残秋露冷,胭脂井坏寒螀泣。到如今,惟有蒋山青,秦淮碧。

①六代:公元三世纪到六世纪约三百年间,先后有吴、东晋、宋、齐、梁、陈六个王朝建都于此。

②王谢:东晋时期的重臣宿将王导和谢安,二人皆居乌衣巷。

③乌衣巷:在南京市秦淮河南。

The splendour of the Six Dynasties①
Gone with the passing of spring,
And no more heard of again.
In vain I look with regret at the mountains and rivers
And all the well-known places,
But they are no longer as in the past.
Two swallows play before the former houses of Wang and Xie,②
In the Lane of Black Uniformed Guardsmen,③
And look familiar.
Late at night I hear the rising tide
Surging still against the lonely citadel.

---

① Between the third and the sixth centuries, the Wu, Eastern Jin, Song, Qi, Liang and Chen Kingdoms made Nanjing their capital.

② Two powerful families, that of Wang Dao and Xie An, had their houses in Nanjing.

③ The Lane of Black Uniformed Guardsmen was where these two powerful houses of Wang and Xie were situated.

六代繁华春去也,更无消息。空怅望,山川形胜,已非畴昔。王谢堂前双燕子,乌衣巷口曾相识。听夜深,寂寞打孤城,春潮急。

思往事,愁为织,怀故国,空陈迹。但荒烟衰草,乱鸦斜日,玉树歌残秋露冷①,胭脂井坏寒螀泣②。到如今,惟有蒋山青,秦淮碧③。

①玉树:即《玉树后庭花》,曲名,为陈朝国君陈叔宝所作。

②胭脂井:在南京鸡鸣山南。陈亡,陈叔宝为躲避隋兵,与爱妃张丽华匿藏于此被俘。寒螀(jiāng 将):蝉。

③蒋山:即南京市紫金山。

When I think of the past
My mind is beset by many sorrows.
Only traces left of those former kingdoms
In ruins amid the mist and withered grass.
The sun sets and crows fly in confusion;
No more the song about jade trees and flowers in the back court. ①
Only the autumn dew grows chill,
Only the ruins of the Rouge Well, ②
As the cold insects chirp and weep.
But the Jiang Mountain remains green,
The Qinhuai River remains azure and serene.

---

① The king of Chen had a favourite song sung by his favourite concubine Zhang Lihua.

② When the Kingdom of Chen fell, the king and his concubine hid themselves in this well, but were discovered.

这首词抒写羁旅思乡之情。上片写奔赴山海关中途夜宿军帐时的苦闷,下片抒思乡之情。语言和谐明快,感情表达率直自然,风格缠绵哀惋,是纳兰性德的代表作。

山一程,水一程,身向榆关那畔行①。夜深千帐灯②。

风一更,雪一更,聒碎乡心梦不成③,故园无此声。

①榆关:即山海关。那畔:那边。

②帐:指行军扎营用的帐篷。

③聒(guō 郭):喧扰,嘈杂。乡心:思乡之心。

Over mountains, over rivers
We plod to the Shanhai Pass.
A myriad of fires light the night
From our camp on the river bank.
The shrieking snowstorm breaks my dream
Of my peaceful, tranquil home.

如梦令(万帐穹庐人醉)·纳兰性德(1655—1685)

"万丈穹庐"、"星影摇摇"首二句勾画出一派寥廓气象,而"人醉"、"欲坠",已知非燕赵豪雄之作。归梦本已难成,而异乡梦回,更是凄清。即令如此,仍是再向梦中觅故园之路,数十字之中,蕴有四层意思,直是情深之作。

万帐穹庐人醉①,星影摇摇欲坠。归梦隔狼河,又被河声搅碎②。还睡,还睡,解道醒来无味③。

①穹庐:圆形的毡帐。

②"归梦"二句:是说家乡远隔狼河,但能梦中归去,而河声彻夜,搅得不能成眠,连归梦也做不成。狼河,白狼河,即大凌河,发源于辽宁省凌源县,东流到锦县入辽东湾。

③解道:知道。

290

The vast encampment is locked in drunken slumber.
The stars whirl and whirl, as if to crash to earth.
Dreams of return blocked and crashed by the Bailang River.
Sleep on! Sleep on!
To wake would be too doleful and too drear.

己亥杂诗(其一百二十四)·龚自珍(1792—1841)

全诗表面上是对风神、雷神和天公的赞颂和祈求,实系借题发挥,借用"万马齐喑"比喻清王朝政治腐败,扼杀人才,到处死气沉沉的情况,反映了作者强烈要求改变社会现状的思想。本诗是代表诗人思想和风格的名篇,是现实主义和浪漫主义有机结合的一篇佳作。

九州生气恃风雷①,
万马齐喑究可哀②!
我劝天公重抖擞③,
不拘一格降人材④。

①九州:中国古代分为九州,后用以作为中国的代称。恃(shì市):依靠。

②万马齐喑(yīn 音):语出苏轼《三马图赞引》:"时西域贡马,振鬣长鸣,万马皆喑。"这里比喻当时社会令人窒息的沉闷局面。喑,哑。究:毕竟。

③天公:即玉皇,神话传说中的天帝。抖擞:振作。

④格:规格。

Our whole land needs wind and thunder to revive it,
Sad it is when all coursers are mute;
I beg Old Man Heaven to bestir himself
And send down talents of more kinds than one.

杞人忧·秋瑾(1875—1907)

秋瑾是我国近代著名的女革命家兼诗人。其早期诗多为倾吐个人的离愁别绪。后期,革命思想在诗中纵情迸发,充满了革命家的豪爽激情。本诗即是抒发忧国之情、救国之志的著名诗作。

幽燕烽火几时收①,
闻道中洋战未休②。
漆室空怀忧国恨③,
难将巾帼易兜鍪④。

①幽燕:指河北北部,古代这里是燕国和幽州的属地。烽火:古代边境遇到有敌情就升起火来作为警报,称为烽火。这里借指战争。

②中洋战:指义和团同八国联军的战争。

③漆室:战国时鲁国漆室县有一女子为忧国事而适龄不嫁。这里作者借指自己。

④巾帼(guó 国):古代妇女的包头巾。兜鍪:(móu 谋):古代兵将打仗时戴的头盔。

When will the flames of war be extinguished?
I hear we still wage war against the foreign devils.
In vain I grieve for my country,
Wishing to exchange my kerchief for a helmet.